People-Centered Evangelism

People-Centered Evangelism

John F. Havlik

BROADMAN PRESS
Nashville, Tennessee

© Copyright 1971 • Broadman Press
All rights reserved
Second Printing

ISBN: 0-8054-2518-7

4225-21
Dewey Decimal Classification Number: 269
Library of Congress Catalog Card Number: 74-136130
Printed in the United States of America
5.D7018

This book is dedicated with love and gratitude to my wife, *Anna Mae,* and my daughter, *Brenda.* They have spent many days and nights without a husband and father, so I could help some people find their way back to God.

FOREWORD

People-Centered Evangelism was written by the right person at just the right time. John Havlik's entire Christian experience has been moving him toward the conclusions which are presented in this excellent book. He writes as an experienced and committed evangelical whose salvation has made him begin to feel about people the way his Lord does. In a day when people are used and crushed and pressured, it is good to be reminded that the God of creation who has revealed himself in Jesus Christ is a God who loves persons.

This book will be no comfort to those people who are looking for a respectable way to give up evangelism. John Havlik's whole life and ministry is committed to the fact that it is only in Jesus Christ that men have hope. He contends without apology that the winning of the lost is at the heart of the Church's mission.

This is not a book for those frightened people who are hoping to escape the frustrations of today by making a certain understanding of evangelism their hiding place. Without stuttering, the author focuses the Word of God on the issues of modern man.

The book *is* for that host of people who seek not only to share the good news but to be it. The author, throughout the book, spells witnessing out as being personal. He tries to help us see that learning to genuinely love people is a part of our witness.

This is a book for pastor and laity. I commend it to you.

KENNETH CHAFIN
Director of Evangelism
Home Mission Board
Atlanta, Georgia

PREFACE

The whole mood of our time may be summed up in the word "people." The secular world has discovered for itself the Christian doctrine of man. Some of the goals of new organizations might well be the goals of the evangelistic church. If all the protests against war, poverty, and pollution are made because of a respect for people, they are good signs. It may be that in the discovery of the Christian doctrine of man, our generation may discover the Christian doctrine of God. When Jesus wanted to tell people what God was like, he told them about a "certain man who had two sons." It is imperative to help people see that Christians have always believed that people matter, even though we have not always practiced it.

Youth have become concerned about the church. They are concerned that the church rediscover the Christian doctrine of man. There is evidence that their concern is not in error. Jesus told us that the essence of saving faith is love for God and love for our fellowman. He showed us that this love is to be constant even when man is not lovable. Jesus came so that we could see God in THE MAN. Renewal for the church may come when we rediscover the love of God in our loving sinning and suffering humanity. Revival will come when the church sees man through the eyes of God, and the world sees God through the eyes of man. This is what this book is about.

The word "evangelist" is not used in this book in a "professional" sense. The evangelist is any believer who wants to share his faith in Christ because he is excited about the gospel and his understanding of it. He is so excited; he shares his faith with people. The generation gap and the culture gap are easily breached when the Holy Spirit is the communicator of the gospel. Therefore, there is very little in this book about "how to do it." Our greatest need is not more methods or techniques but rather an excitement about our faith that comes from the Holy Spirit. The chapter "A Book of the People" appeared substantially in *Is the Bible a Human Book?* published by Broadman, 1969.

This book is not written for preachers and theologians, though it is hoped that many preachers and theologians will enjoy it. Methods are not discussed since the church has already more methods than it can use. There are no footnotes or quotations which, far too often, are only a clue to the writer's insecurity. There are only a few Greek and no Hebrew words discussed, though the Greek text of the New Testament has given the author many shared insights. The author is deeply indebted to many books he has read, sermons he has heard, and discussions with others, but the manuscript was written with no book in hand. It is a book for people.

JOHN F. HAVLIK
Atlanta, Georgia
May 10, 1970

CONTENTS

CONTENTS

1
People Matter

No man is an island, intire of itself; every man is a piece of the continent, a part of the main; if a clod be washed away by the sea, Europe is the less, as well as if a promontory were, as well as if a manor of thy friends or of thine own were. Any man's death diminishes me, because I am involved in mankind. And therefore never send to know for whom the bell tolls; it tolls for thee.

JOHN DONNE

It's "blowin' in the wind" that people matter. In the language of youth—that's what the whole scene is about. War is evil because it hurts people. Poverty is wrong because people suffer. People are singing, "What the world needs is love—sweet love, but not for some, for everyone." Many are determined that all people have their share of this "good earth." All of this because people are saying that people really matter. The little people of the earth do not mind being little, but they are weary of being treated as if they are of little importance.

Schools, universities, corporations, labor unions, and even nations have been put on notice. People matter. The church is also being told that people are important. They are saying to the church, "If you want us so we can finance more new buildings or increase the size of your congregation, forget it!" They are looking for a church that is long on love and fellowship and short on finely drawn theological distinctions and preoccupation with numerical growth. They are saying to the church, "Don't tell us you love people while you maintain a policy of racial segregation." They are looking for a church like the one in the New Testament where "there is no difference between Jews and Gentiles, between slaves and free men, between men and women" (Gal. 3:28).

In all fairness it must be said that people do matter to many churches and to many of their members. The church in the past and present has spoken out against beverage alcohol and other social evils because of what these evils did to people. But what were the "big sins" of yesterday are not necessarily the "big sins" of today. Murder on our highways, air and water pollution, racial pride and discrimination, and war may be the "big sins" of today because of what they do to people. The church must not lack courage to declare itself on these social issues.

The church has grounds for suspicion of what has been called a "social gospel." There is a danger that we believe the lie that you can change men by changing their external circumstances. But this well-founded suspicion must not force us into a spiritual isolationism from the issues of life that will undercut our evangelism. The social reformer may try to alleviate suffering without seeing the sin that brings the suffering. The church also is in danger of becoming so obsessed with sin as a principle that it no longer sees suffering humanity.

People Matter to God

The Old Testament is looked upon by most Christians as having equal authority with the New Testament. It is full of passages that indicate that people matter to God. One great teacher of the Old Testament said, "Amos snorted every time he saw a palace." He was a man of the people, a champion of the poor and oppressed. He says that the Lord will never forget those who "buy the poor for silver, and the needy for a pair of shoes" (Amos 8:6a, KJV). What would he have said about physicians who in a few months have become rich on Medicare and Medicaid fees? What would he have said about millionaires who pay no income taxes because they are able to employ clever tax lawyers? He might say: "For I know your manifold transgressions and your mighty sins: they afflict the just, they take a bribe, and they turn aside the poor in the gate from their right" (Amos 5:12, KJV).

Micah speaks for God: "He [God] hath shewed thee, O man, what is good; and what doth the Lord require of thee, but to do justly, and to love mercy, and to walk humbly with thy God" (Mic. 6:8, KJV). Two of God's requirements are social and one of them is toward God. These requirements Micah says are more important to God than formal acts of worship. Jeremiah voices the Lord's judgment upon Shallum and accuses him of robbing working men of their wages, all the while enjoying his comfortable house. He reminds him of Josiah who, "judged the cause of the poor and needy." He then asks, "was not this to know me?" (Jer. 22:16, KJV). He implies that to know God is to be just in our dealings, to be just in the wages we pay, and to be just in our treatment of others.

Do people really matter? God says yes. And God says yes most emphatically on a skull-shaped hill outside Jerusalem. The cross tells us the value that God set upon people. "For God loved the world so much that he gave his only Son, so that everyone who believes in him may not die but have eternal life" (John 3:16). God wanted men to know how much he cares—how much he loves them. God wanted so much for men to know that they matter to him that he did not count the cost. Holiness, righteousness, and power we might have expected of God, but he wanted us to see his tender, self-sacrificing, and generous love. When you substitute "me" for "world" in John 3:16, you have discovered a personal Savior and a God who cares.

Jesus Christ came into the world to preach, to show, and to illustrate the love of God. In his life and in his death he was saying, "This is the way God loves you." Jesus Christ did nothing to change what the attitude of God had always been. He came to tell all of us in speech and action, in life and death that God loves us and has always loved us. He wanted us to know that God knows all about us and still loves us. He came because he believed that those who would truly see the love of God would believe and love God. This is the message and the ministry of the evangelist—to tell men and to show them what it means to love a loving God. The evangelist, like our Savior, believes, too, that once men really see the love of God, they will love God and their neighbor.

People Matter to Jesus Christ

Humanity at its best is evident in Jesus. He was touched deeply by human tears and suffering. If being a Christian is being Christlike, then we want to know what he was like. What thrilling pictures we have of him in the four Gospels! He invites himself home to lunch with Zacchaeus. He joins in the marriage celebration in Cana. He takes time to talk with a woman of bad reputation at the well of Sychar. He becomes angry with the money changers who rob the poor pilgrims in the very sacred precincts of the Temple. He stops and talks to children and says everyone has to be childlike in trust to be truly saved. Jesus took time for people. Many times he did this over the protests of his disciples. He was interested in their lives as well as their "souls."

Jesus has been called "the Man for Others." Everything he did and everything he was verify this estimate of him. Paul tells the Philippians: "And look out for each other's interests, not just for your own. The attitude you should have is the one that Christ Jesus had" (Phil. 2:4–5). He then reminds them in the following passage that Jesus thought only of others and not of himself. He loved others and died for others. He came to restore to others what they had lost, fellowship and communion with God. He could do this because he had fellowship and communion with God. This life that he lived is available to every man through faith in him. He says that every man has a right to have this life. "I have come in order that they might have life, life in all its fulness" (John 10:10b).

The Gospels reveal Jesus as "the Man for Others." He is the champion of the poor. He warns a large crowd of hypocritical church and social leaders who "take advantage of widows and rob them of their homes, then make a show of saying long prayers!" (Mark 12:40a). He treats women in a way that ignores the prejudices of the day. Where he stops to rest or stay, he begins immediately a clinic for the sick and suffering. He places love for neighbor alongside of love for God in true religion. He says that satisfying human hunger is more important than religious customs and rituals. He shows sympathy and understanding for children that is not common to his time. In parables, such as the good Samaritan, he teaches social compassion and racial equality. He insists that care of one's aged parents comes before religious obligations. He declares that being right with one's neighbor is more important than praying and indeed is a prerequisite to prayer. He stretches out a hand of compassion and concern to foreigners who are not a part of the "chosen people." His value judgments of the life of a Christian are in terms of social and ethical standards and not in terms of religious rites or exercises.

One cannot miss the point, however, that Jesus never said or taught that improvements in social conditions would usher in his Kingdom. He made it plain that the coming of the Kingdom was clearly associated with his band of men and those they would win to the Kingdom. They were to be the new humanity, the new social order, who would be the servants of others. He told them that if they wanted to be first in the Kingdom they must become servants of everyone. He said, "For even the Son of Man did not come to be served; he came to serve and to give his life to redeem many people" (Mark 10:45). They were never to be a part of detached religion that imposes heavy religious burdens on people, "yet they aren't willing even to lift a finger to help them carry those loads" (Matt. 23:4b). They were to bring forth fruit that would benefit all men and society. They were to win disciples. This was the way the Kingdom was to grow, not by social improvement.

Some will say that the Galilean never challenged the social order. They have failed to see that the Jewish leaders were the power structure of that day in Palestine. He challenged the social order by direct confrontation. He struck blow after blow at the involved traditions of the scribes and Pharisees. He used the most burning language ever used against them. It must also be said that he never used violence nor incited to violence. He never retaliated. His greatest challenge to the social structure was that people were more important than religious symbols, religious holidays, or religious structures. In the name of God he struck blow upon blow at the scribes and the Pharisees and their encrusted traditionalism. As a result of this, he incurred their undying and unrelenting enmity and ended up on a cross. They were "the establishment" of his day.

People Mattered to the Great Evangelicals

There are many glorious pages in Christian history that fill the heart of the socially aware evangelical with joy. The pages of early Christian history are full of thrilling stories of Christians, who contrary to the spirit of the cruel and inhuman times in which they lived, proved to be a friend to God and man. We mention only one example among many in order to concentrate upon that group called "The Great Evangelicals" of the seventeenth, eighteenth, and early nineteenth centuries. Alexandria was stricken with an outbreak of the plague in the third century after our Lord. The bishop of the church there, Dionysius, tells of the love and devotion of Christians who tended the sick, catching the plague and dying with it. Their pagan neighbors meanwhile fled from their own loved ones throwing them out in the streets to die. At about this same time contrary to Roman law the Christians declared that marriages between slaves and even between freemen and slaves were sacred and legal.

The great evangelicals and revivalists are the spiritual fathers of modern evangelicals. That these daring men and women were conservative in theology and revivalistic in method and social activities is a well-documented fact of history. Brainerd was born in 1718 and in 1743 began his horseback ministry to the wilderness. His evangelistic zeal and fervor are well known to all evangelicals. In 1744 he wrote in his *Memoirs,* "In about fifteen months past I have given to charitable purposes about one hundred pounds." He used a great deal of his income to support a student in Yale. He supported a woman schoolteacher at Kent when he launched a wigwam school. He used his money to block the schemes of white men to foreclose Indian lands for whiskey debts. His successful social experiment at Cranberry Farms illustrates his social action. He built there a school, an infirmary, and a carpenter shop. Brainerd would have to be classed as a mystic, but his evangelism included very practical social concerns.

John Wesley wrote a letter three days before he died to William Wilberforce, encouraging Wilberforce to lead the fight against slavery and the slave traffic. Wilberforce, who was converted enroute to London from France in 1787, decided to enter the ministry but he met John Newton, the former slaver, who urged him to serve Christ in the House of Commons. He struggled for twenty years until in 1807 the bill to abolish the slave trade passed the house, and one month after he died the 700,000 slaves in the British Empire were set free.

Shaftesbury, born in 1801, became a member of the same group of evangelical laymen as Wilberforce. They were dedicated to making Christian faith relevant to the issues of their time. With zeal Shaftesbury went after the running sores of British industry: safer working conditions, the exploitation of the chimney sweeps, lack of medical protection, child labor in the factories, and female labor in the mines. Many bishops and church people opposed his programs of reform. Undaunted by opposition, unawed by wealth represented in the industrialists, and undergirded by his evangelical faith he pressed the battle until the lot of the working man was better and safer.

Charles Finney left his law office in 1821 and became "the father of modern evangelism." He began a school for evangelists. The town of Oberlin grew up around that school. It became a main connecting point on the "underground railroad." Finney himself hid slaves in his attic. Some of the professors of the school were jailed for getting a slave out of the hands of a United States marshall. His deep sense of social commitment was exceeded only by his evangelistic zeal. He was a tireless speaker, addressing antislavery society meetings over the state of Ohio. He may have meant as much to the cause of the Negro as Garrison. He prayed that the gospel he preached would save men's souls, revive the church, and reconstruct society.

In 1900 Mel Trotter opened his mission in Grand Rapids, Michigan. In 1940 he died. On Thursday, September 12, the Grand Rapids Morning Herald carried an editorial about Mel Trotter. The editorial said: "How many men and women Mel Trotter brought to repentance none can ever know. They numbered many thousands without doubt. How many lives he had saved, how many hungry stomachs he had appeased, how many bodies he had clothed, how many souls he had brought to God is a secret of God alone."

Very few evangelicals remember or know of the social compassion of William Ashley Sunday. Every time "Billy" preached, the Bible was open to Isaiah 61:1: "The Spirit of the Lord God is upon me; because the Lord hath anointed me to preach good tidings unto the meek; he hath sent me to bind up the brokenhearted, to proclaim liberty to the captives, and the opening of the prison to them that are bound" (KJV). He gave the entire revival offering ($113,000) from the New York campaign to the Red Cross and the YMCA. In his preaching he advocated woman suffrage, encouraged sex education in high schools, and supported the right of labor to collective bargaining. He taught and preached the equality of the races.

Time does not allow us to tell of all those whose hearts were touched by the grace of God in Jesus Christ and by the needs of humanity. The stories of the social concerns of the great evangelical revivalists, missionaries, and laymen are many and thrilling. There is no greater need than for the evangelicals of today to have a rebirth of social conscience. The other two choices are unthinkable. If we take the gospel and ignore social concerns, we become right-wing reactionaries. If we take social concerns and campaign for social justice without the gospel, we become just social workers without the "bread of life" for hungry humanity. We must take both the gospel and social concern. Indeed as we have already shown, social concern is inherent in the gospel. We will take some risks in this position. There are many who believe that anyone who is socially aware is a pink or a homosexual. There are others who believe that anyone who is an evangelical Christian is an obscurantist with no relevance. These are risks we must take if we want to be Christian and true to our evangelical heritage.

Do People Matter to Us?

There are no easy answers as to how the evangelical Christian will give evidence of a Christlike compassion for humanity. One can make a social issue a god. Some have made the race issue, birth control, or war a test of Christian faith. With some, one cannot be a Christian unless he gets in the marches or joins an Anti-Vietnam war demonstration. The gospel still has no price on it and is for sinners. In the words of teen-agers today, "nobody's perfect." But this does not give us a ticket for indifference. If we cannot join the organizations or marches, we can work for the integration of a neighborhood and live in it. We can help our church open its doors to everyone. We can get in some social programs, such as remedial reading for children. We can practice love for neighbor in particular situations. We may not burn our draft cards, but we can hate war. We can believe that it is wrong for a nation to enjoy prosperity and certain men to get rich on the profits of war. Above everything we can be Christlike.

2
The Voice of the People

*In the best sense of the word, Jesus was a radical . . .
His religion has been so long identified with conservatism—often with conservatism of the obstinate and un-
yielding sort—that it is almost startling for us sometimes
to remember that all of the conservatism of his own
times was against him; that it was the young, free, rest-
less, sanguine, progressive part of the people who flocked
to him.*

PHILLIPS BROOKS

What are the people saying today? It would be well for us to
listen if we want to reach them with the message of the love of
God in Jesus Christ. Listen to the songs the youth are singing.
They are not all trash. Listen to the goals of new organizations
that are fighting for civil rights and social justice. Some of these
goals might well be the goals of a new evangelistic strategy. Listen
to some of the socially aware politicians and world leaders. Are
they saying some things that the church and its evangelists could
say better? Listen to the voice of television as it shapes public
opinion and molds national character. Is it speaking out more
clearly for humanity than the church on Sunday morning?

A Cry for Justice

A cry for justice is being heard in the shouting and cursing
of demonstrators; in the crack of the sniper's rifle; in the march-
ing song "We Shall Overcome." The cry for justice can be seen
in the sullen faces of the slum; in the disruptive rebellions on the
college campuses; in the twisted hate on the face of those refused
their part of "the American dream." The cry of justice comes
from the starving children of Biafra; from the slaves of apartheid
in Africa; from the civilians caught in the crossfire of injustice in
Vietnam; from the Barrios in Bogota; from the Indian tribes in
Brazil; from Watts in Los Angeles; from the slums of New

Orleans and Atlanta; from coal miners in Appalachia; from Indian reservations in the western United States.

But what kind of justice do we want? Some are saying, "I want my rights." Others say, "What I want is a square deal." Another one says, "I want equal opportunity." Still others say, "I want equal wealth." But there must be some gnawing doubts about these answers. What are a man's rights? Who will say what they are? What is a square deal? If we had equal opportunity or equal wealth, could we keep it that way? Would some of us squander it, others keep it, and others multiply it? Could we ever begin to decide what is justice? Does justice mean the same thing in the Communist and the free world? Could a black man from a ghetto in New York and a white man from an upper middle-class suburban development in Atlanta agree on what justice is?

God's Justice or Man's Justice?

The question is, do we want the justice of man or the justice of God? Someone will immediately say: "Why bring God into this? We have tried God in the past and some of the greatest injustices have been done by the church in the name of God." They point us to "holy wars" and inquisitions and the neutral stance of the church amid injustices. They say: "No thanks, I'll take the justice of Marx, or of Thomas, or of Beveridge, but not God's justice." But what of man's justice? Has it brought us any closer to justice? What justice is there in England, or Russia, or Red China, or America? At best it is very imperfect. Though there are well-meaning and sincere individuals, vested interests usually have their way. New classes of privileged take their place above new classes of underprivileged. New reasons are discovered for war, for the existence of poverty, and for the exploitation of labor.

Now what about God's justice. Will it be administered by priests or preachers? It is doubtful that the church (except for some individuals in it) has ever practiced God's justice. Men like Francis of Assisi, Wesley, Whitefield, Shaftesbury, Barnardo, Howard, and others since then have been exponents of God's justice but in many cases the churches from which they came disowned them. The church, too, must discover and practice God's justice.

Man does not live by bread alone. That is the key to justice. This is the ground upon which we encounter God. Justice is the basis of the cross. In the cross, God was "just and justifier of them that believe." But the message of the cross—God's justice is that people matter. He came into the world because of a Samaritan woman, a hated tax collector, a member of the Sanhedrin, a woman taken in adultery. This is so simple that it is absurd that it doesn't occur to us. God loved people. We hear over the radio and TV a popular song that expresses this, "People Need People." But we can never know just how we are related to people until we know and understand God's estimate of people.

If we say, "I want my rights, the rest can go hang," or perhaps, "I'm number one, I'm going to watch out for myself," then we deny God's justice. Justice is not something worked out for us by legislation or some rules gotten up by the bosses or the labor unions. Justice is something we are meant to be and be to one another. Justice means treating other people as God has treated you in the cross. Nations argue over the shape of the peace conference table while young men on both sides die. Labor and capital haggle over wages each seeking a place of advantage for the corporation or the union while families go hungry. Blacks and whites offer and counter offer, threaten riots or threaten sanctions, while blood runs in the streets. But America and Vietnam and North Vietnam, and capital, and labor, and whites, and blacks really are not important, it is people that matter.

The Christian faith has something to say about justice. The Christian faith says that we can really never know the meaning of justice until we recognize that there is a justice higher and more beautiful than any we can legislate. What is more, the faith says we cannot discover or define that justice of God until we recognize our own failure and seek God's help to touch in grace our goodness and understanding. The Christian must know that the bent of man to injustice, greed, and oppression has a claim on us all.

"All men have sinned and are far away from God's saving presence" (Rom. 3:23). All of us, of every race, are inclined to want more than our share. What is more, we are willing to ignore the claims of others in order to get it.

Suffering or Sin?

The environmentalist, or idealistic Communist, or dedicated social planner may believe that justice is to attack and eradicate a particular instance or case of human suffering. It might be that a group of men may not have opportunity to work because of occupation or race. Action against this injustice is important and required. He believes that legislation will accomplish his goal. He begins by bringing pressures upon the power structure in one way or another. Right-to-work laws, fair-housing laws, and other social legislation has been passed in this way. This is right and ought to be. His motive is to eliminate human suffering. Since we all believe that God in a general way is against human suffering, we feel quite sure he is on our side. He is the one that is not sure that we need to bring God in on that at all. But he cannot be sure that the injustice he rights today will not go wrong tomorrow. One slum is cleared and another is growing. Vested interests eat away at the legislation. But the real mistake is ignoring the central claim of the Christian faith that there is a higher and more beautiful justice and that we need the grace of God in Jesus Christ to touch our powers of goodness and understanding to practice God's justice.

Is the real enemy suffering or sin? The cross relates sin and suffering in a dynamic way. Sin brings suffering upon God's innocent. But we must do more than attack the suffering. One greedy landlord may grow rich on substandard housing, but to eliminate the suffering by having his houses razed for a park will not eliminate the greed in his heart. Are we working to eradicate the suffering or the sin? No justice will be lasting that does not change the hearts of men. Are we attempting to reach higher levels of security, creature comfort, and happiness and ignoring liberty, trustworthiness, truth, and justice?

Now I really have dragged God into this, haven't I? But how

do we come to see and know God's justice? How does God change our hearts so that we are become alive to God's justice? The first thing that happens to us is the discovery that we have really done something mean to someone else. Perhaps we hear one of our friends saying, "I really never thought he would do anything like that." Perhaps it occurs to us then that we really never thought we could do such a thing. It can never go beyond this and many times it doesn't and we are soon prepared for a worse evil. But it can proceed to a second discovery—that I have hurt someone else, perhaps someone quite innocent. I have hurt a person, and I am awakened to the fact that people matter. In this stage of awakening, I can see that my injustice has wronged persons who trusted me. It may have been someone quite helpless, a child, a worker, a slum dweller, or a youth. I have hurt someone who cannot help himself. Then like a stab of excruciating pain comes the words of the Savior, "I tell you, indeed, whenever you did this for one of these poorest brothers of mine, you did it for me!" (Matt. 25:40*b*).

The evangelist has a responsibility to help men see that they are sinners in the sight of God. It is for this very reason that evangelism must cry out against injustice in society. Man is not only responsible to God for personal sin but also for the sin of society. A corporation executive can come to feel the sin of air and water pollution as well as the sin of adultery or covetousness. A person living in white suburbia may feel quite smug about personal morality, until the prophet points out that he is a part of a social group that discriminates against a man made in God's image. We cannot escape the fact that Jesus, the Hebrew Prophets, and great Christians since biblical times have felt moved by their evangelistic imperative to challenge the social order and become the conscience of the society of their day.

Love and Justice

The gospel contained an energetic social message and its preachers heralded not only individual salvation but social reformation. It was not only social reformation on that great and final day of reckoning but reformation here and now. Yet one will look in vain for a program of social reform in the gospel. This is true because the program of Jesus is, "Love your neighbor as yourself." These words are made to apply to the world of war, poverty, and injustice. In the story of the last judgment, Jesus made the final test dependent on love expressed in deeds toward one's neighbor. In the story of the rich man and Lazarus, a man's failure to express love in deed was the final indication of lack of preparation for eternal life. The message of the gospel though strongly individualistic is also social. The gospel establishes the individual value of every human soul and love for one's neighbor as the essential feature of its character.

One of the great problems is the communication gap that exists between the theologically trained mind and the mind of the laity in the matter of the relation of love and justice. Those who are trained in the use of the biblical languages know that the "God kind of love" in the New Testament is quite nonemotional. The laity attaches to love sentiment, emotion, and even romanticism. So many Christians think that they can love someone even while they are treating them or allowing them to be treated unjustly. They might have a feeling of affection for a black servant and at the same time be taking advantage of them in the way of wages. They suppose that because they "feel right" toward them that they are loving them.

A church congregation can "fool themselves" by separating love and justice. I know of a congregation who dismissed with a few weeks' notice a pastor who was within a few years of retirement. He had served the church long and well. While he was having surgery for eye cataracts, they dismissed him. When asked about this, they replied, "We loved our pastor, but the church just wasn't going forward." Not even a great corporation would have acted so unjustly toward an employee. We have not seen that it is not a matter of love and justice, or love or justice, or love against justice. Love is justice.

There are many distinctions that attempt to show the relation between love and justice. Love is emotional and justice is nonemotional. Love is of the heart and justice is of the will. Love cannot exist without justice; and justice cannot exist without love. All of these simply reflect the poverty of the English vocabulary. One cannot say that he loves people without acting justly toward them or supporting justice for them. The great evangelicals such as Howard, Shaftesbury, Wesley, and many others had no problem in condemning social injustice and supporting legislation for social justice in the same breath with the gospel. Their fling into the social arena was done in the name of love that is synonymous with justice. Love is not "feeling." Love can be commanded but feeling cannot. No one could say "until death do us part" if love is feeling. One cannot predict his feeling. God expects more of us than a feeling of affection. He expects his kind of love and this means that we will desire and seek our neighbor's welfare and well-being. We can fool ourselves and even lie to ourselves about our feelings, but acts and actions are out in the open.

Jesus said, "A new commandment I give you: love one another" (John 13:34*a*). He also said, "Whoever does not love me does not obey my words" (John 14:24*a*). Jesus talked about love in the terms of obedience and commandment, not in terms of emotion or feeling. Jesus does not want us to feel affection for him, but he desires acts of the will that indicate obedience. This is his social program. It is not directed toward one of our neighbors, but all men. When one man asked Jesus who his neighbor was, Jesus said that one good example was a Samaritan. But the Jews despised the Samaritans. Jesus is saying to us, love your neighbors, all of them. In this parable Jesus placed love in terms of acts and deeds of mercy rather than emotions or feeling. This is his social program and we must neither evade nor avoid it. It is quite probable then that an evangelist preaching in West Virginia who really felt love for people might speak out for Christ and black-lung legislation.

Are We Listening?

"The children of Israel sighed by reason of the bondage, and they cried, and their cry came up unto God by reason of the bondage. And God heard their groaning, and God remembered his covenant with Abraham, with Isaac, and with Jacob" (Exodus 2:23b–24, KJV). God heard the cry of the people for justice. Can we hear the voices that are crying today. The black man crying for civil rights and for justice. The youth crying out against the injustices of the war in Vietnam. The hippies crying out against the emptiness and frustration of modern life. The poor crying out for a share of the plenty that exists all around them. The common man resenting the increased interest rates that are supposed to combat inflation but succeed in making rich bankers richer. God has heard their cry as he heard the cry of his people in the past. But God needs a Moses. Moses hears their cry, too, and puts himself—reluctantly, perhaps—but puts himself in the hands of God.

The Christian has no easy answers to these great problems. He has no special revelation on social issues. The Christian has Christ. Evangelism is the answer, but it will be evangelism that has heard the cry of the people. Evangelism is to call society to repentance for its unchristian acts and consequences and to present Christ as the hope of the world. But this does not excuse us for taking a stand on the side of justice in action and word. Hating every injustice and crying out against every evil, the evangelist preaches "the gospel of the Kingdom of God." He knows, also, that the laws of justice for the kingdom are in the Sermon on the Mount. He takes these seriously.

3

The People's Revolt

Who is so low that I am not his brother?
Who is so high that I've no path to him?
Who is so poor that I may not feel his hunger?
Who is so rich I may not pity him?

Who is so hurt I may not know his heartache?
Who sings for joy my heart may never share?
Who in God's heaven has passed beyond my vision?
Who to hell's depths where I may never fare?

May none, then, call on me for understanding,
May none, then, turn to me for help in pain,
And drain alone his bitter cup of sorrow,
Or find he knocks upon my heart in vain.

S. RALPH HARLOW

Jesus Christ and Karl Marx were both dedicated to change. Change is revolution. The "revolution" was everything to Karl Marx and "the Kingdom of God" was everything to Jesus Christ. The difference was the goal of the revolution and the means by which it was to be accomplished. Karl Marx was interested in revolutionary change in society. Jesus Christ was interested in revolutionary change in man as an individual and in the Kingdom of God. For Karl Marx the instrument of change was to be creative tension in revolution. For Jesus Christ the instrument of change was to be love for God and for neighbor incarnated in Jesus Christ and in the believer. Love for God and neighbor was to be illustrated and made flesh in the "new society," the church. Jesus Christ was a revolutionary.

One hardly needs to say that this is the age of revolution. Youth is in revolt against the establishment that defies the dollar and crowns the computer king. The "hippie" subculture revolts against the meaningless existence "rat race" in the concrete jungle. Children revolt against the hypocrisies and prejudices of their parents. Parish clergy are in revolt against the traditionalism of their denominational hierarchy. Taxpayers are in revolt against the waste and corruption in government. Young medical students are in revolt against the restrictive and oppressive powers of the AMA. Housewives are in revolt against high prices in the local supermarket. The poor are in revolt against the high interest rates and oppressive practices of some slum landlords.

How we shall right these wrongs is the point at which we have divided ourselves into two factions. Some cry out with Marx that the "whole bag" is changing man's social environment. Others insist that everything would be right if man's heart would be changed as an individual. It is either changing man's heart by regeneration or changing man's environment through social reconstruction. Jesus Christ would have agreed with Marx and the present revolutionaries that injustices exist and that changes need to be made. However, he probably would tell again the parable about a man who sweeps his house clean and then lets in ten devils worse than the previous occupants. A Stalin is as evil as a Czar and a Castro as demonic as a Batista. Substituting one set of sinners for another will not solve society's problems. Christ came to change men through a "new birth," but he also came to change the world. He expected men whose hearts had been changed to band themselves together to help change the world by preaching and living a gospel of revolutionary change.

Since we are living in an age of revolution, it would seem that the church believing in a revolutionary Christ, proclaiming a revolutionary gospel, and living together in a revolutionary fellowship would be doing rather well. To the contrary the church is the victim of the worst kind of credibility gap. The world finds our message unbelievable since they are hard pressed to see it illustrated in our lives and the life of the church. When they see the church, they see an institution almost alienated from the goals of humanity. The church has spawned a veritable plague of "radio preachers" who play on the prejudices of people with their "gospel of hate." They are more anxious to maintain the racial and economic status quo than they are to represent the Christ who loves sinners. Young people find it difficult to trust a church that is against the social changes they believe are necessary.

A Revolutionary Kingdom

It is interesting that the gospel is "the gospel of the Kingdom of God." It is the Kingdom which in the purposes of God will replace all the false kingdoms of men which make glittering promises to erase all injustices but because they ignore man's alienation from God soon fail and fall. Because it intends to succeed all earthly kingdoms, the Kingdom of God is revolutionary. The three modern anti-christs, kingdoms of communism, scientism, and existentialism, rightly see in the Kingdom of God a real threat. At times these kingdoms use the symbols and vocabulary of the Kingdom of God. However, they like all other kingdoms will fall and "the kingdoms of this world will become the Kingdom of our God and his Christ." It is his Kingdom and needs no man's protection or preservation.

The Kingdom is God's power and authority evidenced in the whole creation. It is his reign in the lives of Christians where Christ is Lord. It is the final defeat of evil and his reign on the earth as he reigns in heaven. It is the Kingdom for which every Christian prays. It cannot be entered or even seen without an inner change that crucifies self and makes Jesus Christ Lord. "Except a man be born again he cannot see the Kingdom of God" (John 3:3, KJV). "Except ye be converted . . . ye shall not enter into the kingdom of heaven" (Matt. 18:3, KJV). The first Russian cosmonaut that went into space, on his return to earth, said that he did not see God anywhere in space. Our first astronaut came back from space and said he saw God everywhere in space. Neither of them lied because a man cannot see the Kingdom of God without a birth from above.

People need both personal salvation and social justice. The need of people for social justice arises out of man's alienation from God. In short the problem is sin. The gospel of Jesus

Christ is always addressed to individuals, but it is more than a message to individuals. It is a message about how an individual can have peace, joy, and eternal life. It is also a message of hope for the human race. It was, and is, relevant to the needs of communities, cities, and nations. The gospel means deliverance from self and is an individual salvation. There is no other way of salvation. The ones who repent of sin and believe in this eternal life find themselves involved with others. They acquire a new social conscience. The church in the New Testament, like her Lord, soon became involved with the human problems of hunger and suffering.

The social order is involved in the good news for it is the good news of the Kingdom of God. Jesus began his ministry by preaching the gospel of the Kingdom of God, announcing, "The right time has come . . . and the Kingdom of God is near!" (Mark 1:15a). Jesus introduced most of his teachings in parables by saying, "The Kingdom of God is like. . . ." Putting his words into an inclusive command for all who would follow him, he said, "Give first place to his Kingdom and to what he requires, and he will provide you with all these other things" (Matt. 6:33).

The Kingdom of God was here when he came. It becomes more completely here with the addition of each new "citizen" to it. It will come in its fulness at his second advent when all the kingdoms of this world become the "Kingdom of our God and his Christ." To enter the kingdom is to have freedom from the slavery of the world of self-centered interests. The new citizen of the Kingdom must be willing to be involved with the family of God and commit himself to a share of the burdens and joys of the brotherhood.

A very good translation of the phrase "Kingdom of God" might well be "God's social order." Sometimes evangelism has not really seen the full significance of the necessity of commitment to the fellowship. This is quite apparent in the writings of Paul and especially in the epistle to the Ephesians. In chapter 3, Paul says he is the steward of the open secret of the nature of the church-body as the "new race." He says that he is responsible for taking the good news to the Gentiles, "and to make all men see how God's secret plan is to be put into effect" (Eph. 3:9). The saving message includes not only the good news of Christ but also the good news about the church-body, nonracial fellowship of believers whose greatest interest and love is the Kingdom of God.

Men today, as always, are separated by denials of our human unity. National aggressiveness, prejudice of color, class distinctions, and economic forces are all serious continuing problems of humanity. To accept Christ's mind and to enter the Kingdom is a revolutionary experience because one cannot bring these evils into the Kingdom. They may, however, be present in local churches. What is even more revolutionary is that in God's social order love replaces compulsion and forgiveness replaces revenge. Weary world leaders say there is no hope for peace unless the spirit of man is changed. What a time to proclaim and illustrate Christ the Redeemer.

One can see how important this is for evangelism. Men must not be allowed to receive a message about personal forgiveness and enter on a new life without knowing its ethical and social imperatives. Men must be told that to become a Christian means loving one's neighbor as oneself. It means forgiving as well as forgiveness. It means reconciliation rather than retaliation. It means loving one's enemies and doing good things for those who do evil things to you. Instead of telling people how easy it is to become a Christian, we must tell them what the Savior did: "Go in through the narrow gate, for the gate is wide and the road is easy that leads to hell, and there are many who travel it. The gate is narrow and the way is hard that leads to life, and few people find it" (Matt. 7:13–14).

A Revolutionary Gospel

Jesus proclaimed the Kingdom "at hand" in his own coming. It was present in his own life and ministry upon the earth. It is here and now for everyone who receives him as Savior and Lord. It will come in its fulness by a climactic act of God in

32

human history, the second coming of Jesus Christ. It is God's "social order" and it does proclaim social justice, but only regenerate sinners enter into it. Most churches are full of people who have never entered the Kingdom. The failure of the average church member to bear witness to the transforming power of Christ is a clear sign that they have never experienced his redeeming grace and transforming power in a "new birth." Indeed, the major problem in world evangelization may not be the indifference of the world and the hostility of the enemies of the gospel but rather the unevangelized members of the church.

The way and gate into the Kingdom are narrow and only a few find it. Our gospel is so revolutionary that most revolutions are tame when compared to it. No other revolution proposed as a cure for the ills of humanity faces the fact of sin. The world needs a revolution far more radical than that of communism, scientism, or existentialism. They only call for a change in the externals of man's existence. The gospel calls for a change in each man. Our gospel says that God by a mighty act came into the world in Jesus of Nazareth who was born as no man was ever born, who lived a sinless life as no man has ever lived, who died for our sins in a death such as no man ever died. By the supernatural birth of Jesus Christ and the "new birth" of those who repent of sin and receive him as Lord and Savior, a "new humanity" was begun.

Conversion means that a man is changed. But it is not just the externals of his life that are changed. Conversion is "turning to God" but it is also "turning from self." When self is crucified at the center of our being and Christ is enthroned there, our lives can no longer be the same. Too many times going to church, leading in prayer, tithing, and reading our Bibles are taken as the definitive signs of conversion. A truly biblical view, however, would make unselfishness, forgiveness, compassion for others, kindness, love, joy, and peace the most definitive signs of Christian conversion. One can be real religious, but only end up being a "religious stinker." The credibility gap of Christians widens when non-Christians observe in our fellowship petty jealousies, the spirit of retaliation, racial prejudice, and animosities. Evangelism thrives when Christian conversions heal old prejudices, resolve old rivalries, and change old, bad attitudes.

Conversion is only the beginning of Christian life and growth, and regeneration is the birth of the "new born babe." When Christ comes into a person's life to live as Savior and Lord, one does not become, as if by magic, suddenly a perfect Christian with no more temptations or problems. In some instances some things essentially evil have become a part of a "Christianized culture" and they are not eradicated easily. Those who taught and preached the gospel neglected to declare the whole gospel for the whole man, and evils were tolerated too long. Implications of a "new birth" were not explained and too often not lived. In some instances mental assent and emotional experience were not accompanied by miraculous, spiritual transformation. Conversion aims not only at a new man, but ultimately at a new world. The prophets described that world when men shall beat swords into plowshares and the lion sleep contentedly and peacefully by the lamb.

The statement is often made, "The best way to change the world is to get people converted." Though this has a great deal of truth in it, it is a serious oversimplification. The Bible, itself, does not promise this. Indeed, the Bible is quite clear that society will not be truly converted until the Kingdom of God comes upon the earth. It is well to remember also that a man who has been born again, who has experienced Christian conversion, must grow in Christlikeness and grace. In the new truth in it, it is a serious oversimplification. The Bible, itself, possess the potential for such a life in Christ. Given proper Christian nurture and teaching, he will respond in Christlike living. The power of sin has been broken in his life. It need no longer have dominion over him. Evangelists do not remember that Ephesians 4 says that they have been given to the church "to train the saints to do the work of serving." The New Testament evangelist has a much greater responsibility than "getting people down an aisle."

34

The evangelist has the joy of witnessing to the power of a revolutionary gospel. It is a gospel with dynamic power to change men. Think of the slave trader, Newton, who became the writer of gospel songs. Think of Augustine, the sensual pagan, who became the author of *The City of God*. There are men today who are being changed by the power of the gospel. We can witness to its power with confidence when we have experienced its transforming power in our own lives. As Bob Dylan sings, "The answer, my friend, is blowin' in the wind." Jesus said to Nicodemus, the intellectual, that the new birth was like the wind. You cannot explain it, but you can feel its effects and observe its power. May the wind of the spirit blow across our disillusioned, disturbed, and doubting world as men of the spirit preach the gospel of transforming grace!

A Revolutionary Church

A crowd of people came down the street of the city dragging along with them two disheveled men. The crowd is yelling as they come to a precinct station, "These troublemakers who have been making trouble in other places have come here." The serenity and security of the city was threatened by these outsiders. Did this happen in Atlanta last week? No, it happened in Thessalonica in Macedonia 1,019 years ago. The two apprehended men were Christian witnesses named Paul and Silas. They had been witnessing to the gospel of salvation. They were preaching love. They had healed sick people and befriended the poor of the city. They were just acting like Christians are supposed to act. They never said a word about politics, business, or the social order. Indeed, they had urged their followers to "obey the authorities" and to honor the magistracy. Real Christianity does hurt evil politics, or evil business, or evil social practices.

There is plenty of social revolution in the gospel of Christ. The gospel lived and applied hurts business—the liquor business, the drug business, the slave business, and the "rich richer and the poor poorer business." One of the earliest charges against the church was that "they hurt business." Paul's gospel operation in Ephesus was so successful that it was hurting the "god-making business." The silversmiths got up a mob and tried to lynch Paul. Evil business has always operated the same way. You please the appetites of some demonic craving, build up a clientele, then raise your prices. "Easy credit" and high interest rates today are good examples along with the drug traffic. It may be significant that one of the charges leveled against the early church was that it was not good for business and today generally the economic power structure believes that churches are "good for business."

The thing that is disturbing is that so few churches (even the avowed evangelical ones) have a revolutionary ministry. Where is the evangelism of a local congregation so changing the lives of men that evil business and evil men see that church as a threat to their existence? It is quite true that this is still happening in isolated instances, but the incidents are far too few and scattered. One cannot take the New Testament seriously without believing that evangelism and the church cannot be torn apart. But beyond any question the real "hang up" in evangelism is the local church. Even denominational literature designed for the local church talks about missions and evangelism as if they are options for specialists who "want to do their thing." We cannot plead our lack of numbers or of funds. When compared to the infant church of the first century, we are like a mighty army. We have everything except the evangelistic zeal and enthusiasm necessary for world evangelization.

One of our problems is our obsession with programs and buildings. Modern denominations can boast of computerized programing, but they lack apostolic power. The only obsession of the church must be missions and evangelism. In the early church, if a person were not a witness, he would stand out in the church as different. Today, if someone does get a "magnificent obsession" for witnessing, the rest of the church looks at him like he is "some kind of nut." One evidence is the large number of church members visiting for the church, inviting people to the classes and organizations, and perhaps no one really witnessing to the saving power of Jesus Christ. Christ has promised to "build the church" if we would be faithful in our witness to Jesus Christ as Lord.

Another serious problem in having a revolutionary church is that we have not trusted the lay people with the gospel. The church suffers seriously from the clergy-laity heresy. Most pastors do not believe that they can trust their people with the gospel. Most of the time in planning for lay evangelism and witnessing the first and most serious bottleneck is the clergy. There may be a built-in fear that the laymen may "take over the church." This is observed even in some very evangelical pastors. A professional church staff is paid to do evangelism in all too many churches. This is especially true of the youth. No one is better equipped to win the high-school generation than the college youth, but very few churches are really "turning their youth loose with the gospel." A lot of "dumb games" in the church basement will not challenge the youth of our generation to serious commitment to Jesus Christ. A "brotherhood supper" or "church knife-and-fork club" will not "set on fire" the men of the church.

It may be that we need to ask ourselves if it is possible that the lack of a revolutionary quality in a local church may not be because very few of our people have really been radically changed by a New Testament conversion. Why are so many college students reared in the church abandoning their faith? Why are so few of our church members interested in evangelism? Why has our standard of a "good Christian" become a matter of church attendance rather than faithfulness on witnessing? Why do so many of our church members retain so many anti-Christian racial attitudes and "hang ups"? Can it be that our most fertile field for evangelism is the members of our churches. A good prayer might be, "Oh, God save us from ourselves!" The church, being a revolutionary fellowship witnessing to a revolutionary gospel, and living in and looking for a revolutionary kingdom, ought to be the most exciting thing in the world.

4
Let My People Go!

Good critics who have stamped out poet's hope,
Good statesmen who pulled ruin on the state,
Good patriots who for a theory risked a cause,
Good Kings who disembowelled for a tax,
Good Popes who brought all good to jeopardy,
Good Christians who sat still in easy chairs
And damned the general world for standing up—
Now may the good God pardon all good men!

ELIZABETH BARRETT BROWNING

Moses was the liberator of his people. He saw his people as slaves in bondage and his whole life was changed. He could not enjoy any more the pleasures of peaceful coexistence with Egypt. Jesus saw people in the same way. Coexistence with the powers of the world that enslaved man was an impossibility with him. He challenged these powers, and they hung him on a cross. On the cross he prayed the greatest prayer ever prayed, "Father, forgive them; they know not what they are doing." He never for a moment forgot human responsibility which he taught clearly. But this prayer reveals that he saw these people about to murder him as caught in forces beyond their control. He came into the world as liberator (redeemer). He came to "set us free."

The evangelist must be more than a messenger of liberation, he must be a liberator. At this point the gospel touches social compassion in an intimate way. The note of joy so apparent in the apostolic gospel and so absent in modern witness arose out of this liberating power of the gospel. The evangelist must be identified with the physical and social needs of the people. The powers that enslave man spiritually are given expression in those powers that enslave man physically and socially. Alienation from God expresses itself in greed, prejudice, pride, and inordinate ambition. These are expressed in air and water pollution, extortionate interest rates, high medical fees, et al. It will be much easier for black Christians who identified with the civil rights movement to evangelize their people than it will be for those who "sat out" the struggle of their brothers for justice.

The gospel is relevant to the need of modern man as it has been for men in every year since the first century. Man's basic need is liberation. What are people saying today? They are saying, "I want to be free." Freedom from drugs, from boredom, from alcoholism, from sickly obsession with sex, from the "rat race," and from resentment and hate. They are saying, "I want to be loved." They want to be accepted as they are and for what they are. They want recognition, a sense of belonging. The youth are screaming at us, "I want to be heard." They even sing dolefully about people who listen but never hear us. Why can't we who are Christian understand that our gospel is speaking to this very need? The early Christians preached and lived freedom from personal "hang ups" and social pressures.

Negative morality homilies and good advice must not be mistaken for gospel witness. The world hears us saying, "be good," or "don't do this or that." They are already as good as they can be and they are tired of the restrictions that society imposes upon them. In Jesus Christ Christians possess that very thing that man wants and needs. Instead of hearing from us the joyous message of "the glorious liberty of the children of God," they are bombarded with ecclesiastical "hang ups" and theological controversies and a lot of good advice. One preacher says everyone must be baptized by his denomination to be saved and another preacher says you don't have to be baptized at all. Even our protests against social evils usually take the form of stern denunciations of people instead of an expose of what some evil does to people made in the image of God.

People in Bondage

A verse poignant with compassion and pregnant with concern looks into the loving heart of God with incredible insight. "I have surely seen the affliction of my people which are in Egypt, and have heard their cry by reason of their taskmasters; for I know their sorrows" (Ex. 3:7, KJV). God wants no man made in his image to be a slave. In spite of this incredible love, man in his rebellion is a slave to the very creation in which God made him lord. All the wonderful gifts of God including work, sex, and inter-personal relationships have been so twisted and given over to demonic powers that they have become the instruments of man's enslavement. What scientific discovery has man made that was not first made in the interest of war and man's inhumanity to his fellow? Modern medicine has given us drugs that are about to destroy us. Man unlocked the secret of the atom. Has this secret been used for the blessing of mankind or is it the ominous cloud hanging over us?

Are we hearing the cry of people in bondage? Hear the anguished cries for help and hope that are coming to us in what people say and sing. See the living dead wearing the faceless mask of anonymity on the streets of our great cities. Feel the despair that hangs like a pall over the teaming slums. Experience the emptiness in the heart of the suburbanite riding his power mower over his lawns. Compassionate the alienated kid next door smoking his first "joint." Understand the anguished cry "God help me" from the dirty girl who looks like an old woman in a slum apartment with three dirty kids whimpering in hunger and her man "long gone." Isn't this what Christians are supposed to feel, and hear, and experience? What are they saying and how does our gospel relate to their cry?

They are saying, "I want to be free." They call it "doing their own thing." Man in rebellion against God has forsaken his freedom. He turns from God to other things to express what he thinks is his freedom. He knows cigarettes cause cancer, but he continues to smoke. He knows high-powered automobiles pollute the air, but he continues to burn rubber to the delight of Detroit. He knows drugs can blow your mind, but he continues to use them. Driven by what he thinks is nemesis or fate toward his own damnation he cries out for freedom. He cannot see in the lives of very many believers the freedom he longs for. The youths wonder why their Christian parents object to their use of pot or speed when they are hooked on tobacco and tranquilizers. It is time that we Christians understand that it is not enough to preach a great gospel and a great Savior. We must begin living great lives.

Isn't this the greatest time to say, "Man, Christ can set you free." The gospel alone can help a man to the freedom to say no to the things that would enslave him. To be redeemed means to be set free. The wonderful thing about Christ is that he helps us "to do our own thing." Indeed, only in him can we find the power for self-realization. This is our gospel. He breaks the power of canceled sin and sets the prisoner free. It is not strange that in the synagogue at Nazareth he read, "to preach deliverance to the captives, . . . to set at liberty them that are bruised" (Luke 4:18, KJV). To our hooked generation we must say out of personal experience, "Christ can set you free." We must tell them that Christ does not save a man to enslave him. He does not confront us as a moral teacher and practitioner and say, "Try and be like I am." He comes into our lives and helps us be what we ought to be. Neither does he expect "instant perfection." He is neither shocked nor surprised by our weakness.

People want to love and be loved. They want to be accepted and respected as persons as they are. Many teen-agers want their parents and teachers to accept them as they are, not as their elders want them to be. With the terrible "mess" we have made of the world, isn't it a little strange that we do want to "make them in our image." With all this hue and cry for love, why doesn't the church answer with a demonstration of love? But the world sees in our personal and corporate lives as Christian a terrifying lack of love. Radio preachers make the networks blue with their attacks on fellow Christians. Fights in local assemblies of Christians receive wide publicity. Christians say loveless words of prejudice and hate. The world devises its own version of love that gets all mixed up with sensuality.

Have Christians ever had a better opportunity to witness to Christian love? We must help men see that the cross is the greatest demonstration of love in human history. The love-light of Calvary has never fallen upon most people, because they have never seen it demonstrated. "Behold how they love one another" was the greatest public relations of the apostolic church. The world isn't impressed by buildings, or programs, or pulpit ability, but men know love when they see it. We cannot say, "God loves you," unless we can say and demonstrate, "I love you." It would be well for us to remember the words of John in his first epistle, "And this commandment have we from him, That he who loveth God love his brother also" (John 4:21, KJV). To love and be loved is not only a basic need of people, it is also the heart of the gospel of Christ.

People not only want freedom from bondage and freedom from loneliness, but they want freedom from guilt. "I want to be clean," is a basic need of man as a sinner. After a gospel meeting one night, I talked with a woman who felt dirty. She wondered if God would accept her. She was burdened with guilt for a sinful, wasted life. I told her that God loved her like she was and wanted her to come to him. I told her about forgiveness in Jesus Christ. We knelt in prayer and she gave her heart to Christ. When she stood to her feet, the first words she spoke were, "Preacher, I feel so clean." The *Playboy* philosophy of gratification of all desires to find release and peace is a fraud. So many who embrace this philosophy try to drown their guilt in alcohol, or drugs, or suicide. Only Jesus Christ can forgive sin and wipe out guilt.

I Am Come Down

God said to Moses, "I am come down to deliver." Those of us who know the gospel see this as a foregleam of the condescending love of God in Jesus Christ. He came down and lived among us. He wept our tears; he felt our loneliness; he knew our despair. He identified with us and became the "captain of [our] salvation made perfect through suffering" (Heb. 2:10, KJV). He did not even look upon his eternal deity as something to selfishly keep for himself but became a man and lived among us. God's

42

strategy for evangelism was identification with us in our sinfulness. An old English Christmas Carol sees the advent purpose clearly and sings, "The holly bears a berry as red as any blood, and Mary bore sweet Jesus to do poor sinners good." He did not come to condemn, but to save. "The Son of man is come to seek and to save that which was lost" (Luke 19:10, KJV). "God was in Christ reconciling the world unto himself" (2 Cor. 5:19, KJV).

Moses, himself, became a liberator when he saw his fellow Jew being beaten by an Egyptian. A militant was born by the injustices of Egypt. But God knew that militancy doesn't deliver. It enslaves. Those who take up the sword, perish by the sword. It is much easier, however, to admire the militant than those who "sit out" the struggle for liberty. God took the hot-headed militant into the desert where amid the pastoral surroundings he made peace with God and with himself. Then at the foothills of Horeb, God revealed himself in the burning bush and in a holy experience the hot-headed militant became the hot-hearted evangelist. God filled with zeal and compassion the heart that had been filled with zeal and hate. In this experience Moses identified with his people and with their struggles. He gave up being called a son of Pharaoh's daughter for the position of a slave.

Doesn't this give us a clue for an evangelistic strategy for the church today? It is to dream the impossible dream and right the impossible wrong. The "theology of involvement" had an insight at this point. It is unfortunate that some of the advocates of this thought adopted the weaknesses of the world. One doesn't need to add cursing to his vocabulary to communicate with the world, but one must add loving identification to communicate. The Christian and the church must be identified with the basic needs of man. One of the things that may have changed the thinking of Ezekiel from an emphasis on the wrath of God to an emphasis on the mercy of God is his experience that he recounts, "Then I came to them of the captivity at Telabib, that dwelt by the river of Chebar, and I sat where they sat, and remained there astonished among them seven days" (Ezek. 3:15). It makes a difference when you sit where they sit!

An ordinary church member may look at a sad situation of a person's enslavement to vicious habits, or dangerous pride, or grinding poverty and lament that it is like this. The committed Christian looks at the same situation and believes that it can be changed by Christ. It is at this point that he becomes a liberator. He comes down into the human situation. In this time of loving condescension, the Christian is Godlike. The greatest danger is that we should "come down" as an act, as a supreme hypocrisy, in order to evangelize rather than coming down into the human situation out of Christlike love. All of us can come down into the misery of some life with compassionate love, introducing Christ who sets men free. We can get involved in the hopes, fears, and tears of people. The church must find ways to get its members involved with people.

A Christian is a "Christ-one." It may be that we have a lot more church members than we have Christians. Christ came down into the life of man and got involved. How few of the professing Christians have ever been involved in the lives of others! The problem is then, how do we make Christians? The obvious answer is that we cannot make Christians out of people. Only Christ makes Christians. It is our task to "preach Christ." This will mean that we will spell out what commitment to Jesus Christ means. It means a cross. It means death. It means the funeral of self. It means that we are now committed to serving Christ by serving others. The evangelist cannot make Christians, but he can spell out what becoming a Christian means. Peter's answer at Caesarea Philippi makes it clear that it is the business of the evangelist to testify that "Jesus Christ is Lord." Then he promises to build the church. We have been far busier "building the church" than testifying that Jesus Christ is Lord.

Confronting Old Pharaoh

God said to Moses, "Go tell Pharaoh to let my people go." Moses answered, "Who, me?" This is the identical response of most Christians today when they are reminded that we must not only confront evil in the life of the individual but we must confront evil in the social order. It is true that the power that enslaves man is demonic and that the problem is a spiritual one, but these demonic powers are often epitomized in "power structure" in the social order. One example which ordinarily finds sympathetic hearing with evangelical Christians is the liquor traffic. We are against liquor because of what it does to people made in the image of God. But almost all evangelical churches contribute and work in organizations that have lobbies in state legislatures and in Washington. We know that in order to combat the liquor traffic we must "confront Pharaoh in his palace."

The whole concept of the kingdom of God and a new earth are indications of God's concern for the social order. God not only loves me but "God so loved the world." Laymen who are Christians and serve as officers of a corporation can be helped to see that it is a sin against people for their corporation to pollute the air we breathe and the water we drink. Christians who are lawmakers and politicians can be helped to see that it is a sin against people to discriminate in the matter of civil rights or jobs against people because of their race. Because men do something together in society which is against the interest and well-being of people does not make it right. Banks advertise that the "rich man's" dollar is worth 7½ percent interest while the "poor man's" dollar is worth only 4½ percent. Is this justice? Does a Christian have some responsibility as an officer of a bank for this injustice? An automobile salesman who hides interest rates and "fast talks" a young couple into debt beyond their means has sinned against people.

When we confront such evils as these we will be misunderstood. We will be called "crusaders" and perhaps even "militants" when all that we have done is to raise our voice against the evil long entrenched and very profitable. We will be accused of "getting into politics." They will remind us of "the separation of church and state." Those same people will say, however, that this year they will give their minister a larger amount of his salary in housing allowance rather than a salary raise. They see no inconsistency in letting Uncle Sam pay their minister's salary increase. For people like this there is very little hope and very little indication that they really are Christian at all. The evangelist, because he loves people, will protest every evil that makes their life harder and their burden heavier.

If we protest this concept for a moment, may God help us remember the Hebrew prophets and Jesus the greatest prophet of them all. The evangelist will be pressed, living in an increasingly computerized and mechanized world where every thing militates for the depersonalization of man. People are increasingly manipulated and used by government and big business. Many church-related investment funds really need to give up their shares in some of the repressive finance companies. The conscience is dulled when we operate as a corporation or as a state or federal agency. Many times, in order to secure the release of slaves from bondage, we will have to confront old Pharaoh in his palace. May the Lord help us to do better than, "Who, me?"

5
The Church Is for People

The church is never a place, but always a people; never a fold but always a flock, never a sacred building but always a believing assembly. The church is you who pray, not where you pray. A structure of brick or marble can no more be a church than your clothes of serge or satin can be you. There is in this world nothing sacred but man, no sanctuary of God but the soul.

Anonymous

Is the church for people or people for the church? This question speaks to local congregations. Do we want people for the sake of a larger church with larger buildings and a larger budget? A church leader of a white church in a racially changing community commended the congregation for a large offering saying, "thank you for your gifts. This shows everyone that we are determined to keep this building (heavily mortgaged) open." Is this what the church is for—to maintain buildings out of sentimentality or is it to minister to the people of the community? This same church decided (just before it died and went out of existence) to not advertise its Vacation Bible School that year because "some of them" might come. It deserved to die. The world was better off when it died.

This was quite a contrast to another church where I was leading in revival services. A very poor woman with a large ill-clothed (and ill-smelling) family had been attending the revival. When I gave the gospel invitation, this woman came forward for church membership. She was the only person who came that night. The pastor afterward said: "that was a good service. I am so glad she came. We can do so much for that family." This expressed the real spirit of New Testament evangelism. A passage in Mark's Gospel is very revealing in this regard. This passage is quoted today to prove that Jesus was a nonconformist, but its meaning is much deeper than that. The hungry disciples were rubbing the heads of wheat between their hands and eating the grains. They were hungry. The Pharisees objected because it was unlawful to thresh wheat on the sabbath. Jesus reminded them that David had eaten the "holy bread" from the Temple and had given it to his hungry men to eat. It was done in the name of human need. Then Jesus said, "The Sabbath was made for the good of man; man was not made for the Sabbath" (Mark 2:27). Jesus was consciously placing humanity above all institutions, religious or secular. Man, he said, is the purpose for which the state and all its social institutions exist.

Jesus or the Pharisees?

Really it comes down to the question, "will our evangelism be the evangelism of Jesus or the evangelism of the Pharisees?" The weakness of the Jewish religious establishment, epitomized by the Pharisees, was that they had the people serving religion instead of religion serving the people. From every standpoint of outward judgment the Pharisees were "good" churchmen. They tithed not once but three times. They were faithful to every rule of their religious order. They were defenders of the written revelation. Their religion was a "load" and not a "lift." As long as religious tradition was observed to the letter, they had no regard for people. They had ready answers to all the questions, but they had no answers for the human heart and soul. People did not matter to the Pharisees.

The Pharisees moved heaven and earth to maintain and build an institution. Jesus died to reach people with a saving message. For the Pharisees it was Judaism, but for Jesus it was people. The Pharisees "moved heaven and earth" to make one proselyte, but they ignored the needs of people that were all around them. The church that is for people is not as concerned about "additions to the church" as it is for the souls, bodies, hearts, and minds of people. Numbers can become an obsession with a denomination as well as a local congregation. It is easy for pastors and denominational leaders to suppose that "their group" will be the only instru-

THE CHURCH IS FOR PEOPLE

ments of God. In this case success is made equal to numerical and financial growth.

A church that I have known for over thirty years was once located in the inner city. It was known far and wide as a great gospel church with social compassion and evangelistic zeal. Hundreds of people were converted and their lives were dramatically changed. People by the hundreds were rescued from the evils of poverty, alcoholism, immorality, and the other social evils common to every great city. They grew affluent. Some of the converts were able to move to nicer homes in the suburbs. The old factory type building no longer suited them. They began to put pressure on church leadership to go to the suburbs. They built a plant costing over a million dollars in a better neighborhood. The life-changing ministry is gone. They are busy making proselytes of other Christians in the suburbs to pay their great debt.

The Pharisees said, "Come," and Jesus said, "Go." The Pharisees wanted people to come to them, to the Temple. For them the center of religious activity was the place of worship, the Temple or the synagogue. For Jesus the center of activity for the faith was in the streets. If Jesus Christ returned to earth as he came in his earthly ministry, he might attend the services of one of the churches. But if we wanted to find him, we would probably have to look in the slums where he would be holding some dirty children on his knee and talking to the family about the Father's love for them. The Pharisees said, "Come to Jerusalem. Come to the Temple. Come to us." Jesus said: "Go. Go into all the world. Go to all races. Go to men in need. Go and witness."

The practice of many churches and much of our church program says, "Come!" Without question, Christians need to come for worship, for training, and for reporting what God has done in the streets and shops. The church in the New Testament met for worship, remembering the deeds and words of our Lord. This seems to have involved prayer, preaching, teaching, believer's baptism, and the Lord's table. The church then moved out to the streets, the shops, and the marketplaces. This was the "as-you-go-preach" emphasis. The church met also to hear testimonies and reports of what God had done in the streets, and shops, and marketplaces. New believers who came with the witnesses were baptized and instructed having been won through the personal testimony of Christians.

The Pharisees were interested in outward and verbal conformity to what they considered orthodoxy. Jesus was interested in the devotion of the heart to God and in a new spirit expressed in love and forgiveness. He reminded people that the summation of all previous revelation from God was: "You must love the Lord your God with all your heart, and with all your soul, and with all your strength, and with all your mind; and, You must love your neighbor as yourself" (Luke 10:27). When the lawyer quoted this, Jesus said, "do this and you will live" (Luke 10:28b). The Pharisees were real sticklers for a set of religious rules. One can get around rules, and they were experts at it. The one rule of Jesus was love for God and for our fellowman. This was the indisputable evidence of conversion for Jesus.

Conversion is turning to God. The evangelist must be careful to not equate conformity to a creed or a set of rules with conversion. There is a danger in attaining mental assent to a "plan of salvation" with which most people of religious background agree and making this conversion. This is the risk many Christians run when they present such a plan in the manner of contracts. Many times when agreement is reached on the three or four points of the plan, the Christian says: "Now, you believe all that, and the Bible says if you believe that, you are saved. Now, thank God for your salvation." Although persons can be genuinely converted on such a presentation, many can also be deceived and confused. It must be made clear that conversion is turning to God in Christ and that it means we will now love God and follow Christ.

The church must decide what it is for. It exists for more than building an institution or an organization. It exists for more than the creation of a "religious ghetto." It exists for more than to serve as a repository of a creed. It exists for more than the maintenance of its clergy. It exists in the name of God and in the name of Jesus Christ for people. It exists for the salvation, happiness, and well-being of people. It exists to prophetically hold the life of man in the light of God and his revelation of himself in the Bible and in Jesus Christ. It exists to preach the gospel of the Kingdom of God. It exists to witness to what God is doing in the life of man. There are some great words in the New Testament that tell us in what way the church is for people.

The Church Is Sharing

The church is *koinonia*. This great word has been translated as fellowship, or association, or community. The simple word is sharing. The focus of this word is on the congregation. The community of believers belongs to the new age and it is the new race. It belongs to the Kingdom. When the church is sharing, its witness is clear and powerful. The New Testament gives testimony to the effectiveness of the sharing community as an evangelistic force. When the church in the book of Acts loved one another and became a sharing community, many people were added to its number. That the church took this word seriously is evidenced by Luke's words, "All the believers continued together in close fellowship, and shared their belongings with one another" (Acts 2:44).

Koinonia means to give yourself to another. The church does not just share. The church is sharing. The New Testament church was not a class church nor was it a racial church. Because of this, it could illustrate *koinonia*. Some of the literature on the church today seems to say that there is some special virtue in an inner-city church and some special evil in a suburban church. Really they are both class churches and for the most part racial churches. The church needs both the rich and the poor, both the Jew and the Gentile. The church in the great city has the best opportunity to achieve this, because in the city the rich and the poor, the blacks and the whites live together. For the church to deliberately go out and get a few poor people and a few black people would be ridiculous and even hypocritical. But for the church to exhibit *koinonia* in the streets so that the poor and the people of other races would know that they would be welcome and wanted is another thing. It is evangelism.

The way that the poor and the minorities are treated in a community is a sign of God's presence and action. The sign of the Messiah was: "the blind can see, the lame can walk, the lepers are made clean, the deaf can hear, the dead are raised to life, and the good news is preached to the poor." The present realization in our nation of the need of the poor and the rights of minorities is a witness of God at work in society. How unfortunate that the church lags behind unbelievers in seeing God at work. What a refreshing breeze of evangelism would sweep this land if our churches were sharing. The church is an illustration of the Kingdom. If the poor or minorities are not welcome in our churches, they may suppose that they are not wanted in the Kingdom.

We may say, "but they are welcome, they just will not come." But what does our architecture and our music and our preaching say? An ordinary working man was invited by his friend to attend revival services when I was preaching. The auditorium cost over a million dollars. This man told me afterward that when his friend came into the sanctuary, he looked around and said, "Man, I don't have any business in here." Buildings ought to say *koinonia*. Music in most Protestant churches does not speak the language of people. It is for the most part outdated and out of touch with the city where most of our churches exist. Our buildings say, "Don't come in here unless you are clean and well dressed." Our music says, "Don't come in here unless you appreciate 'good' music."

The Church Is Ministry

The church is *diakonia*. We will be quick to recognize "deacon" in this word. It is translated both service and ministry. The Gospel of Mark is rich in *diakonia*. The men who enrolled in the Master's school took lessons in *diakonia*. He showed them the running sores of humanity as he drew back ragged garments. He did not flee from the lepers, he touched them. The focus of this word is on the laity. In the rural and uncomplicated life from which we came, the layman was a pew-sitter and at the most a member of a church committee. If the faith is to spread today, it will have to be spread by the laymen. The insipid religious education we have offered laymen will have to be replaced by rigorous training in serving. The Master girded himself with a towel and washed the disciples' feet to example this life of service.

The whole program of the laity serving is in the words of Jesus, "In the same way your light must shine before people, so that they will see the good things you do and give praise to your Father in heaven" (Matt. 5:16). This means more than becoming super-intendent of the Sunday School, although that is a good thing. It means that one will be serving God every day in his work or profession. We could restore a good biblical word to the vocabu-lary of the church, "apostolate." The church sees itself continuing the apostleship of our Lord upon the earth and in the world. Most laymen (and pastors have encouraged it) see their life in the church as spiritual and their life in the world as secular. But the layman in the apostolate of Christ sees himself as a servant for Jesus' sake. It is serious to break with the church. It is also serious to break from the world—to withdraw from it—ignore it.

The ordained clergy might ask, "What is my place then?" The pastor must be the guardian of the faith and the interpreter of truth. Ephesians 4:12 says that the ordained clergy are to "train the saints to do the work of serving" (Author's free translation). The layman is in the front of the battle, on the cutting edge of the faith. He is there to serve in the name of the servant. The task of the clergy is to equip the layman for the work of serving. He is the servant of the laity. He is an illustration to them of what they ought to be to the world. He is their minister to teach them to minister. He is loving, compassionate, forgiving, and self-effacing to teach them what they ought to be in the world. Through the laymen, the church will be involved (serving) in the arenas of society for justice, freedom, and compassion. The clergy will set goals and determine objectives. The laymen will have the tech-nology to make the goals attainable.

The Church Is Proclamation

The church is *kerugma*. The focus of this word is on the or-dained ministry. The *kerugma* is the proclamation that the Kingdom has come in Jesus Christ. We proclaim by sharing and serving as well as verbally. In a special sense, however, *kerugma* is the faith verbalized. The symbol of the faith is the Pentecostal tongue of flame. There is a danger that we think in modern terms of advertising or propaganda. The propagandist makes men into his own image through the use of personal stories and testimonies. There is very little of this in the New Testament. *Kerugma* is the gospel preached and lived. *Kerugma* makes the message of the Bible live in terms of today. It is not vain repetitions of creedal statements but a living message. To illustrate, the parable of the good Samaritan goes like this: A white Christian lady living in a lovely suburban home finds a drunken Negro prostitute beaten and lying in her driveway one morning. Does she call the police and stand peeking out the window until they come and drag her off or does she revive her, help her into the house, put her in one of her beds, and take care of her until she is well? If she does what Jesus would have done, she is *kerugma* in sharing and serving. The modern urbanite can understand this parable.

The message of the gospel proclaimed must never become a dull recital of the history of salvation but a thrilling message of freedom. Our evangelism would be much more effective if the preaching of the message were in the language of the people to whom we preach. Many a workingman sleeps through the Sunday morning service, not because he is so tired, but because he doesn't know what is going on. Those who preach publicly must work at putting the *kerugma* in an understandable framework. Rural illustrations and rural stories do not communicate to the "now" generation in the cities. I cannot believe that the spoken message has lost its power. I do believe that in many cases it has lost its relevance.

Evangelism in the New Testament sense means that the church is for people. The church cannot rely solely upon the spoken message. The message of the gospel must be proclaimed in sharing and serving. In order for the church to do this it needs to have a new focus on the congregation as sharing or *koinonia*. There needs to be a new focus on the laity as serving or *diakonia*. The ordained ministry must find its primary function in motivating and training the laity for serving. The place of worship and training and reporting is the place of worship. The places of witnessing and serving are the streets, the shops, the factories, and the business houses. This is the "new" evangelism that is just as old as the New Testament.

6
The People's Church

*I should like to see Christian leaders disregard their
timid followers and like Francis of Assisi or John Wesley
go out of the church buildings, shake the dust of de-
nominationalism from impatient feet, and appeal to the
folks generally. Americans will listen to religion if and
when it claims to have relationship to real life. Let the
churches recognize that their job is not to nurture the
pious nearly so much as it is to rouse, convict of sin, and
convert a pagan nation.*

BERNARD IDDINGS BELL

A people's church is a church that has trusted the laity with the
gospel. In far too many churches evangelism is a task that is con-
ceived as being the task of the clergy. The average church seeks to
entertain its youth with a lot of "square games" in the church
basement and to keep the interest of its men with a "knife-and-
fork club" in the fellowship hall. In spite of all the protests of the
clergy against the lack of involvement in evangelism on the part
of the laity, the clergy continues to structure a church program
that makes their involvement almost impossible. Most church activities are designed to bring people into the church building. The
degree of involvement in these activities are the standards by which
a Christian's commitment is measured. Being a good church member often obscures the necessity for being good Christians.

To take seriously the command of Christ to evangelize the
world is to face squarely the fact that the world cannot be evangelized by the clergy and the church professional staff. There are
far too many people without Christ for the clergy to be successful
in world evangelization. The modern church must become the "lay
church" of the New Testament. Many of today's evangelistic organizations that are outside of the local church report that the
greatest barrier in organizing the laity for an evangelistic crusade

is the clergy. Pastors say that their people simply will not do "the work of an evangelist." When the people are organized into witnessing teams and trained as personal counselors, many pastors are amazed and even puzzled. Sometimes they are even critical of the evangelist who has the people doing what they were not doing in their local church situation. The truth is that someone has come along who is willing to trust them with the gospel.

Most lay persons are quite convinced that everything the church does is evangelism and by serving on church committees, teaching classes, or singing in a choir they are "doing their bit" for evangelism. Evangelism is making Christ known in such a way that each person confronted is faced with a personal decision about Christ, a clear yes or no. The mission of the church is to carry out the will of God in the world. The broad view of the task of the church is mission, but the cutting edge of mission is evangelism. Anything that works toward the carrying out of the will of God in the world is a part of mission, but evangelism is confronting persons with the gospel and the opportunity to make a decision. The Christian has an obligation to contribute to the mission of the church, but he also has an obligation to operate on the cutting edge, to evangelize.

There are people who are hungry. That kind of hunger is not right nor is it the will of God. To feed them by being a conscience for society in crying out against injustice and to minister to them personally is my mission and the mission of the church. In the same way there are people who are sick or the victims of discrimination or injustice. This is not the will of God. It is my mission and the mission of the church to help them in the same way. There are persons who are alienated from God who need the gospel and an opportunity to respond to it. Giving them the gospel and an opportunity to respond to it is evangelism. It is the cutting edge of mission. Communists, too, help and heal and teach, but only Christians evangelize. Because they teach, heal, and help does not make the Communist mission Christian. They are humanitarian in many cases. The Christian also must be humanitarian, but the focus of

57

the Christian is on purposive witness to man's deepest need, his need of Jesus Christ. Only evangelism makes our mission Christian.

The word "evangelism" is unfortunately given a professional meaning in the modern church that it never had in the New Testament. It is in too many cases equated with "preaching." The angelic choir over the field of the shepherds sang the good news. The good news may be sung, whispered, printed, taped, discussed, reasoned, and communicated in "sign language." Indeed, the best word may be "communicate." Many times the language of the common man is far more communicative than the technical language of the clergy in communication of the gospel. Evangelism is action. In too many churches "talking about evangelism" is evangelism. Evangelism is not a theory, it is action. In a great evangelistic conference in which I was speaking, we were really busy inside the great church talking about evangelism. One pastor full of inspiration went out on the streets and in two hours he returned with a man he had led to personal faith in Christ. He brought the man to the platform. The man gave his testimony. We were talking about evangelism, but this one man was doing evangelism.

The word "ministry" has also lost its New Testament meaning in many churches. To most church people today the word ministry is synonymous with the clergy. Everyone who is a Christian must be included in the ministry. The idea that lay people are to help the clergy does not go far enough. Indeed, the New Testament idea is that the clergy exist to help the laity (Eph. 4:11–13). The lay people are exposed to the life of the world and they must be equipped to transform it by Christian witness. This does not make the professional ministry unnecessary as the anticlerical movement declares. It makes the professional ministry highly necessary to the success of the lay ministry. A danger is that we create "professional laymen" who are imitations of the professional clergy. These men become great speakers on lay witnessing when they are far away from home where the people do not know that they seldom, if ever, involve themselves in a personal ministry to people.

Our desire to return to what the early church did in evangelism must not arise out of a slavish preoccupation with the methods of the New Testament. We should study the methods of the early church because they were successful in evangelism. In the purpose of God and out of centuries of experience, we should have advanced far beyond what they did. Our present failures in evangelism in the light of their successes ought to drive us to study what they did in evangelism. It probably was not their methods that made them successful but rather their commitment to Christ and involvement in evangelism. These are the things we must imitate. Of one thing we can be sure, the church is not the faithful coming to a hallowed shrine by the thousands, but rather a company of believers sent out two by two to witness publicly and from house to house.

The Worldly Church

The first strategy of the people's church is that of involvement in the world. The church is in the world. Soon after the first century the church began to withdraw from the world. The monastic life became the ideal of Christian virtue. Even among evangelicals the doctrine of "separation" involved withdrawal from the world. Most "good Christians" were notoriously poor members of labor unions, P.T.A.'s, or social clubs. Opportunities to meet persons and confront them with the gospel were sacrificed on the basis of piety. There evolved a breed of Christians who were "so heavenly minded they were no earthly good." Involvement with non-Christians was almost totally in arranged situations, such as visitation programs. Many times the witness was limited to invitations to attend Sunday School classes or revival meetings. This worked fairly well as long as the church had a monopoly on the social contacts of the community, and this kind of arranged witnessing may be effective in some communities today. It would have been out of touch with the first-century world. It is certainly out of touch with most of the world in which we are living.

The church should remember it is not "of" the world. It must not forget it is "in" the world. The everyday contacts of human life are the best platforms for Christian witness. The church must be made up of redeemed people who carry their witness for Christ into the common life of the community. The church must witness to the invasion of time by eternity in Christ. The witness must be carried out in the world of men. This strategy calls for involvement in all the orders of human life, the school, the clubs, the athletic teams, the charity drives, and so forth. The Communist strategy of penetration and subversion is the very strategy employed by the church of the first century. They penetrated the army and even Caesar's household. The church on the offensive must carry the witness to the gates of hell. He has promised that those gates would not prevail against us.

This strategy would not destroy the meeting place, the home base. Indeed, it makes the center of fellowship more important and more needed. Returning to the warm fellowship of the home base will be needed after strenuous ministry in the field of operations. The shock troops of invasion will need to return regularly from the field of operations. They will return for sharing sacred experiences of God's work in the world; they will report, they will learn, they will fellowship, and they will worship. Strengthened, they will return to the world for more penetration. If this seems to be too militant in its discipline, read carefully the passages in the New Testament that reflect military discipline. This kind of discipline might cause some churches to lose rather than gain membership. It would on the other hand increase our evangelistic effectiveness and power.

The concept of a worldly church calls for a fresh and exciting concept of the ordained minister. Big churches are big business and ordained ministers tend to become big businessmen. The concept of the worldly church calls for an ordained minister whose first concern is "equipping the saints for the work of ministry." He is a player-coach. His primary concerns will not be the administration of the church as a big business nor the staging of a weekly religious show for spectator-saints. His concern will be to inspire, motivate, and involve fellow ministers (though not ordained) in a ministry of witness by penetration in the world. He will surround himself with a professional staff who have expertise in equipping saints for ministry. This concept would call for a new concept of training men for the parish ministry. Theological schools have really been a dismal failure (with a few exceptions) at this point. Now that the successes of the church are few and scattered, the layman who has had only a spectator stake in the church is free to criticize.

The Witnessing Church

Another needed strategy for the people's church is to make the gospel intelligible and believable for the people. A pastor in a Sunday morning service said that our present-day faith must become anthropocentric. A truck driver on the way out asked what the preacher meant by "that long word." Fortunately he asked a Sunday School class member, a denominational theologically trained person, who answered, "He means our faith must be people centered." The truck driver said, "Then why didn't he say that?" Has the church professional protected his position from the threat of the laity by using a special "holy vocabulary?" This babel in the modern church comes from its intellectuals on one hand and from its traditionalists on the other. The intellectuals are guilty of using technical vocabulary and philosophical concepts that cannot communicate to the common man. The traditionalist uses a King James vocabulary which has now lost its meaning to the average person.

At this point, many of the church's theologians have committed treason. They have betrayed the church that supports them. The intellectuals of the church have an obligation to interpret "a reason for the hope within us." This interpretation must be for the masses. Theologians have been largely occupied with adapting the faith for their fellow intellectuals. Pastors coming from theological schools echo the uncertainty that was communicated from their professors. This "fogginess" of thinking that only raises more questions is just as dangerous to the faith as the anti-intellectualism of the ultra-fundamentalists. Our faith was framed not in the philosophical Greek of the schools, but in the "gutter Greek" of the streets and the marketplace. It may be humiliating to us that this is so, but a little humility may help us. Paul tells us in the first letter to the Corinthians that he did not pick his people out of the noble born or the philosophers. Could this be true so that he would have people who would use language that the people could understand?

The layman is likely to communicate the faith in more understandable terms than the ordained minister. It is not an accident that the most vital Christian movements have been those movements led by lay preachers. The first century church, the Anabaptists, the Franciscans, and others were primarily lay-preacher movements. The danger we face in this is that we substitute a "lay clergy" for a professional one. It is not difficult to foresee laymen becoming "great speakers" in "great demand." The church needs articulate laymen, but it also needs the humble and even stumbling testimony of the ordinary man. One of the finest lay ministers I have ever known was a steel-mill man with a fourth-grade education who said, "ain't" and "has did." What he lacked in finesse he made up for in humility and commitment. God used him in winning many of his fellow workers and in a hospital visitation ministry that was effective. His big calloused hand on your arm and the tears in his eyes were better communicators of Christ's love than a good vocabulary or good diction. People had no difficulty understanding him.

The whole matter of communication of the faith must be seen in a new light. It was "tongues of fire" that spread the faith in the post-Pentecost period. God has no "news team" operating on a great TV network. He probably doesn't want one. The reporters are supposed to be men and women who have been touched by his grace and power. The constant lament is that the "good news" never makes the networks. What is more important and pertinent, do we know of very many Christians who are real reporters of good news? Great churches, great revivals, great rallies on full-page ads in the great dailies and television spots cause very little stir in a great city. A great revival crusade may report one hundred thousand in attendance in a ten-night campaign. This is probably not more than twenty thousand different people and most of them church people. What is this in a city of two or three million? But suppose that four or five hundred thousand Christians in Atlanta suddenly become real reporters for God sharing the good news with power and effectiveness?

The Serving Church

The people's church will be a church that serves humanity. This is its third evangelistic strategy. Christ girded himself with a towel and washed the feet of his disciples. Paul says that Jesus Christ took the form of a servant. The Savior reminded us that to be great in the kingdom is to accept the servant role. To accept this role is difficult and hard. Many of us who are pastors and denominational leaders have accepted the name of "servants" of God, of the churches, and of the people, but we have had difficulty assuming the role. In this we can only learn from him who was the mightiest of the mighty and "emptied himself" and became a servant. This role is predominant in the Gospel of Mark. It is clear after careful study that the commission in this gospel is that we go into the whole creation and serve. The servant role is a commitment and an attitude before it is evident in action.

It is quite certain that we cannot assume the servant role for humanity until we have assumed it with one another in the fellowship of believers. We discover a great source of power when we learn to serve one another. Someone has said that large churches are churches where no one knows anyone else and they are glad they don't, and small churches are churches where everyone knows everyone else and they are sorry they do. Though this is an overstatement, there is enough truth in it to frighten us. Some modern church programs give the impression that the people of the church are serving the pastor in carrying out "his program." Deacons sometimes leave the impression that they are "the rulers" of the church. Even Sunday School visitation is sometimes done for "their teacher."

Servanthood is friendliness. Jesus called his people "friends." There are many among the youth of the church who need a friend. Loneliness is the curse of our time. Many lonely people are found in the church. Our conversations are in too many cases dialogues of deaf people, because no one is really listening. The church that is a "society of friends" will find its fellowship attractive and charming. Our openness to persons will determine our success in evangelism. How can we be open with strangers when we do not even know our brothers in Christ? Renewal cannot take place for the church until we "bear one another's burdens." Friendship means that we so identify with someone that their joys and sorrows become ours. Our lives get so mixed up with theirs that we hurt where they hurt.

Servanthood is loving. The love of Christ makes our love of men evident. The greatest argument for the authenticity of the fellowship is not our orthodoxy but our love for one another. It is a tragedy when man and woman live together in marriage without loving one another. It is equally tragic when our lack of love in the fellowship of the church is apparent to everyone. Our evangelism is sure to be ineffective when this is so. Men and women who are living without God will never know his love unless they see that love in us. The great chapter on love in 1 Corinthians was written to a loveless church. As beautiful as it is, it is unfortunate that it was necessary for the apostle to write it. The love of God is believable only when it is embodied in a believer.

Servanthood is caring. We must not be afraid of emotion. Youth is looking for real emotion in their faith. The faith does not need to be framed in mental icicles. A good many church men will need an epitaph that reads, "He died of too much self-control." Our message and our music need to give evidence of caring. When Jesus saw the city with its heartache and its rejection of God, he wept. He cared. So much preaching and so much church music sounds detached from the cares and heartaches of people. An alcoholic in St. Louis came to Jesus Christ. I asked him why he came. He answered: "It was those two deacons. They came to see me every Sunday when I was getting over a drunk. They stood by the bed and talked to me each week about Jesus. I saw the tears in their eyes. Preacher, there ain't nobody cried over me since my Mother died."

7

A Book of the People

When from my eyes no tears will flow,
But all those tender springs are dead;
When any tale or mortal woe
Still leaves unbowed a haughty head:
Aloof in self-complacency,
Then pity me, O weep for me!

When any cry of human wrong
Shall fail to draw me from my path;
Or evil fail to make me strong
With impulse of a righteous wrath:
Dead in my own sufficiency,
Then pity me, O grieve for me?

TERTIUS VAN DYKE

God has chosen to reveal himself in the Bible and in Jesus Christ, "of the people, by the people, for the people." The Scriptures were written in the language of the common people and were written for people to read and understand. People with all their frailties and differences are the instrument of God's revelation of himself. The New Testament was written not in the scholarly Greek of the classroom but in the "gutsy" language of the street. It is rich with idiom, slang, and even curses. The gospel must be witnessed to in the language of the people. This alone is an evident reason for lay witnessing. The seventeenth- and eighteenth-century language of the clergy does not communicate to the common man. "Tell the story simply as to a little child" is good advice not only for child evangelism but all evangelism. No one can understand the great joy in the human heart when one hears for the first time the glorious gospel in simple "people" language.

Only those who have spent years never having heard those words can know the spiritual joy of hearing them for the first time. I was born in Milwaukee, Wisconsin, and lived there until

I was a teen-ager. I never heard the saving words from human lips there. My family then moved to Tulsa, Oklahoma, and there I heard from the lips of three persons witnesses to Jesus Christ as Lord and Savior. From the lips of three Christian witnesses, simple words, about the one who being God became human, and died for me. I made a personal response of trust, commitment, and love to Christ. He made me a witness with the capability of using words, my words, to tell what he has done for me.

My personal experience with Jesus Christ brought a dynamic change in my life. My sister had a similar experience with Christ at the same time. It was then our joy to witness to other members of our family. Today almost every member of our large family is a Christian and is serving Christ. Because we were not familiar with the Bible and could not exactly quote passages of the Bible, our witness was primarily in terms of living and sharing our faith in our own words. It really seems to me that our experience includes all the necessary ideas that relate to our wonderful privilege of bearing witness to the transforming power of Jesus Christ.

Jesus Christ, the Word, as a Witness

Jesus Christ is THE Word. People needed to know what God is like. Words describe what things and people are like. John called Jesus THE Word because Jesus showed us what God is like. Many people feel that God is an angry old man who tells them, "Don't do this," or "Do that." All he does, they think, is to give us orders. This is so apparent in human relations in the home. Some teen-agers never really understand their parents. Distance and alienation are the result. They may go on thinking this until something happens that makes them see that the Father still loves, still cares, and indeed is hurt more by the alienation than they are hurt by it. This is the whole point of the parable of the prodigal son.

We are so far away from God. Our sins build barriers between ourselves and God. We are rebels flying our own flag of self. God wants to say something to us, but we are not listening. Isaiah said it like this: "Behold, the Lord's hand is not shortened, that it cannot save, or his ear dull, that it cannot hear; but your iniquities have made a separation between you and your God, and your sins have hid his face from you so that he does not hear" (Isa. 59:1–2). In one clear, convincing, and climactic word God has said to us what he wanted to say in THE Word made flesh. He came and lived among us. He felt the agony of our loneliness. He wept our tears. He stood in our shoes. He was God with us.

He witnessed to the love of God. Christ never says in the New Testament, "I love you," to anyone. But his love is demonstrated in attitudes and deeds. He loved the poor who came to him. He fed them on occasions. He said it was hypocrisy to go into the home of the poor and say, "I'll pray for you," and leave without giving something to ease the poverty of that home. He loved the sick and he healed them. He was not repelled by leprosy. The cry, "Jesus, help me," never fell on deaf ears. He loved the sinful. The adultery of a woman did not shock him but to her self-appointed judges he said, "Don't throw stones at her unless you have never sinned yourself."

Jesus cared about people. His whole life and ministry are a witness to the fact that God cares about people. It is true that he became angry with the money changers in the Temple. He spoke scathingly of the scribes and Pharisees, but this was always toward religious hypocrisy and never toward people with cares, and sins, and needs. In Christ, God came into the lives of men to share their shame and suffering. God is not just "an angry old man" who issues Ten Commandments from the lightning atop Sinai. He cared about a rich man who had a sick daughter and also about a poor leper. He cared about a chiseling tax collector and a rich, affluent Jew. Is it any wonder that John on Patmos calls him, "the faithful and true witness"?

The Christian witness will want to witness to Jesus Christ, because Christ will show people what God is like. They do not really know God. They are rebellious. Paul in Ephesians says that all of us are "children of stubbornness." The Christian witness should know how to find Christ in the Bible. Philip is a wonderful example for us. Luke tells us in Acts 8 how Philip found the Ethiopian riding in a chariot. This hitchhiking deacon knew how to take the Ethiopian from the fifty-third chapter of Isaiah to Jesus Christ. Andrew and Philip, in John the first chapter, knew how to take Peter and Nathaniel to Jesus from the Old Testament prophecies about the coming Messiah. Someone said of the great preacher Spurgeon that he would take a text from the Bible and beat a path straight to Bethlehem and Calvary. This is a good guideline for the witnessing Christian.

Jesus Christ as a witness came into our world and shared our cares and concerns. The Christian witness can again find a good example in Jesus. One cannot be a good witness if he is aloof from the cares and concerns of people. People are quick to sense a detachment from their problems. If Jesus were here today, he would be a champion of the disinherited, disappointed, and disenchanted persons of our society. The Christian cannot stand aside in the struggle for civil liberties for all, for equal opportunity for all citizens, for better distribution of wealth, and for the realization of the aspirations of minority groups. Men want to know, "Are you really interested in me?" The evaluation of people made by Jesus requires us to be interested in the whole man. The greatest personal evangelists who have ever lived have been those who have identified themselves with the economic, mental, physical, and spiritual needs of men.

The Bible as a Witness

The Bible not only witnesses to Christ but is itself a witness to the saving acts of God and the power of God in the lives of people. The record of the saving acts of God and the testimonies to the power of God in human life are revealed in words. In a special way, these words are given to us in our Bible. The God-given word is basic to both the witness and the hearer of the witness. Without it the witness has nothing to say and the hearer nothing to believe. The Bible cannot be of service to the witness unless he believes that God is its author and that God speaks in the Bible. Perhaps no theory of inspiration can say what one can say in simple faith, "God speaks to us in the Bible through human authors and human words."

The Law is a witness to that ideal that God requires of people. The Law, contained in the five books of Moses, tells a person what he ought to be toward God and toward his fellowman. The Law even went beyond this to laws regarding sanitation and conservation of natural resources. God requires of a person that he ". . . do justice, and to love kindness, and to walk humbly with your God?" (Mic. 6:8, RSV). This portion of the Bible was a witness of the will of God for us. This is what God wanted us to be and do. We cannot know the seriousness of his sin until he knows that he has sinned against God. There is a moral shock for everyone who suddenly discovers the great difference between what he is and what he ought to be in the sight of God.

The books of History are a witness to man's failure to meet that ideal. Book after book records the sad and often sordid tale of man's failure personally, socially, and as a steward of God's good earth. The climax of the self-assertion of man is recorded in Judges 21:25: "In those days there was no king in Israel; every man did what was right in his own eyes" (RSV). Everything one attempts to do without God ends in failure. Isn't this still true of modern man? There is hunger in the midst of the greatest productivity. We are no nearer to clean water and pure air in spite of our technology. The very things that can bring us good housing and the healing of mankind's hurt are turned to instruments of death and destruction in senseless war. Isn't this still true of personal happiness? We have prosperity, better health, and an abundance of food, but are we happy? Divorce, mental breakdowns, and rising incidence of crime say not.

The poetic books of the Bible witnessed to the longing and aspiration of the human heart for God. In spite of all his failures man could not put God out of his life. Especially in the Psalms and in the book of Job this heart hunger comes out in cries to God for help. In Job 23:3–5 the desperate man cries out: "Oh, that I knew where I might find him, that I might come even to his seat! I would lay my case before him and fill my mouth with arguments. I would learn what he would answer me, and understand what he would say to me" (RSV). Ancient man or modern man cannot "kill" God. This longing of the human heart for God is expressed by the psalmist in Psalm 42:1, "As a hart longs for flowing streams, so longs my soul for thee, O God" (RSV).

The prophets witness to the saving power and purpose of God in history. They said that history is really his story and that he would write the last chapter. They inspired hope with the promise of the one who would come and would be the hope and Savior of the world. Isaiah made such a promise in chapter 9 of his prophecy: "The people who walked in darkness have seen a great light; those who dwelt in a land of deep darkness, on them has light shined. For to us a child is born, to us a son is given; and the government will be upon his shoulder, and his name will be called 'Wonderful Counselor, Mighty God, Everlasting Father, Prince of Peace'" (Isa. 9:2,6).

The Gospels witness to the ideal realized in Jesus of Nazareth. The angels sang over the field of the shepherds: "for to you is born this day in the city of David a Savior, who is Christ the Lord. And suddenly there was with the angel a multitude of the heavenly host praising God and saying, 'Glory to God in the highest, and on earth peace among men with whom he is pleased!'" (Luke 2:11,13,14,RSV). He had come, the promised, the longed for one. He came to die. He was everything God wanted us to be. He did not come to tell us what we ought to be. He came to show us and by his life we live. He came as a king, but the king of love. He gave us the laws of his kingdom in the Sermon on the Mount. It tells us what citizens of the kingdom should be and do.

Acts and the Epistles witness to the fellowship of the Christians and their activity in witnessing. Peter and the other early church leaders were asked by the authorities to explain their witnessing activities and they answered, "And we are witnesses to these things, and so is the Holy Spirit whom God has given to those who obey him" (Acts 5:32, RSV). They met for worship, fellowship, and training. They went out into the streets to witness. They returned to the fellowship reporting what God had done, bringing with them some of those to whom they had witnessed. They did not put on religious pageants in which they were only spectators. They were participants in a common adventure.

Revelation witnesses to the final triumph of Christ and his church. In spite of persecution, antagonistic governments, and a lack of strength in numbers they were incurable optimists. They witnessed believing in the final triumph of Christ. They did not sit around bewailing the conditions of the world, they changed the conditions. John saw a new earth recreated and peopled with a new humanity. He said: "Then I saw a new heaven and a new earth; . . . and I heard a great voice from the throne saying, 'Behold, the dwelling of God is with men. He will dwell with them, and they shall be his people'" (Rev. 21:1,3, RSV).

This review of the Bible as a witness can help us see that the witness needs to do more than memorize a few passages of the Bible. It is essential that the witness understand what the whole book is about. I have found that I can use this brief review of the Bible as a conversation with a non-Christian. It will help one to see what God expects of us and how we have failed to meet God's standard. This can explain man's spiritual longing and the awakening of the conscience to failure and sin. Christ is shown as the answer to this longing of the human heart. God has met our need in Christ. The witness of the Bible fills us with an infectious optimism in witnessing.

Saving Faith as a Response to the Witness

In the sixth chapter of John's Gospel, Simon Peter teaches us the nature of saving faith and the meaning of Christian commitment. Jesus had made the claim that he was the Bread of life. To the dismay of many of the Jewish, would-be-disciples he said, in verse 53, "Truly, truly, I say to you, unless you eat the flesh of the Son of man and drink his blood, you have no life in you" (RSV). He later explained that by that he meant the words that he had spoken must be assimilated and become a part of life. Many of the disciples turned their back on Christ and left him. He then asked Peter and the others, "Will you also go away?" (John 6:67, RSV). Peter gave the answer that is the classic answer to Christian commitment, "Lord, to whom shall we go? You have the words of eternal life" (John 6:68, RSV). Notice that it is his words that are emphasized. This certainly includes the Sermon on the Mount.

Christian commitment is believing with all the heart and mind that there is no other hope for eternal life except Jesus Christ. Saving faith is taking all the faith we have out of churches, denominations, lodges, religious rites, good works, and self-righteousness and putting that faith in Jesus Christ who is our only hope. The human witness must himself have made this commitment before he can communicate to others. Peter said in effect, "We have made a choice and there is no going back on it." This is much more than mental assent to the fact that Jesus lived or even that he is the Son of God. The witness is trying to get persons to make a lifetime commitment to Jesus Christ, a commitment the witness has already made.

To become a Christian one must accept his words. To the murmuring disciples after his great claim in John 6:63b he says, "the words I have spoken to you are Spirit and life." He was again explaining what he meant by "eats my flesh and drinks my blood." To accept Christ means that we accept what he said about how to live. Our attitude toward the problems of war, poverty, sex, race, and personal relationships are to be determined by his words. The words are not difficult to understand, but they are difficult for human nature to put into operation. They are impossible without his saving grace. The witness is not just "seeking to save a soul." The witness is interested in the whole man becoming a Christian. The witness certainly has a responsibility to tell those who receive the witness about the words of Jesus that must be assimilated and become a part of life. The witness must make clear to the non-Christian that there is not only a hell to shun and a heaven to gain but A LIFE TO BE LIVED.

The whole issue in personal evangelism is Jesus Christ. He has "the words of eternal life." The witness is seeking an act of the will to make Christ Lord and Savior of life. Our witness is not to the greater desirability of one denomination over another or one religion over another. The witness is to bring men to Christ through the work of the Holy Spirit. Using the words of the Bible, we show them Calvary and the empty tomb. Then we can tell them in our own words what he means to us. Tell them how he changed our lives, our attitudes toward other people, our ideas about marriage, our value judgments about our possessions, and all the other "nitty gritty" of life.

The Christian as a Witness Using the Bible

We have now looked at Jesus Christ as a witness. We have seen him revealed in the Bible. We have discovered that the Bible is a witness to God's holiness, man's sinfulness, and God's grace in providing a Savior in Jesus Christ. But how are we to use the Bible in witnessing to non-Christians? Are we to memorize three or four passages that we call a "plan of salvation" and give it to every person to whom we witness? Romans 3:23; Romans 6:23; Romans 5:8; and John 1:12 are wonderful passages that tell us that we are sinners, that the result of sin is death, that God loves the sinner, and that we need to receive God's Savior. But is this our witness or is it just one of the ways in which we can accept salvation in Christ? God has used such presentations because he has promised to bless his word. But isn't there a better way?

We can use the Bible to meet a person's need. Jesus met the need of every person who came to him. In addition he gave them a personal faith in himself as Savior and Lord. We must not see people as "prospects" to be manipulated, but as persons to be loved by us as they are loved by Christ. One of the most effective personal evangelists I know uses the Bible in a unique way. He uses an incident from the Gospels where Jesus dealt with some person. He uses some incident where similar needs are involved. He then tells the story in his own words, sometimes reading portions from a modern version. He points out how Jesus met the needs of that person and how the person came to saving faith. He then makes an appeal for a decision. I heard him use the incident of Jairus and his sick daughter in the home of a non-Christian couple who had just lost a daughter in death. He ministered to their broken hearts and brought them to personal faith in Christ as Lord and Savior.

We can use the Bible to share God's love and our love. Unless a person can see God's love in us, they cannot understand Bible verses about his love. Love isn't tied to one method. Love finds a way to overcome obstacles. Love is articulate. Love never requires a religious vocabulary. When we can see people and say, "God loves that person and I love him as God loves him," Bible verses come alive. Now we can say, "But God shows his love for us in that while we were yet sinners Christ died for us" (Romans 5:8, RSV), and the words have new meaning and life. We cannot be trained into loving people. Love for people must come through prayer and meditation in fellowship with Christ. Our capacity to love must be cultivated. Paul in 1 Corinthians 13 talked about the emptiness of words without love. Love is always willing to become involved with the needs of people.

We can use the Bible to share the meaning of the cross. The cross is the demonstration of the selfless love of God. Sin is wanting our own way, and having it. Sin is self. The simple and sublime explanation of the death of Christ is that Christ died for me. "I have been crucified with Christ; it is no longer I who live, but Christ who lives in me; and the life I now live in the flesh I live by faith in the Son of God, who loved me and gave himself for me" (Galatians 2:20, RSV). The cross shows us the willingness of God to identify himself with us, even in our sin. The Bible says, "For our sake he made him to be sin who knew no sin, so that in him we might become the righteousness of God" (2 Corinthians 5:21, RSV). The witness will benefit from frequent trips to Calvary. Our greatest enemy in witnessing is self. At Calvary self is crucified.

We can use the Bible in companionship with the Holy Spirit. The witnesses of the early church reminded the questioning authorities, "And we are witnesses to these things, and so is the Holy Spirit whom God has given to those who obey him" (Acts 5:32, RSV). One of our greatest fears in witnessing is, "I will not know what to say, what Bible passage to use." "But the Counselor, the Holy Spirit, whom the Father will send in my name, he will teach you all things, and bring to your remembrance all that I have said to you" (John 14:26, RSV). What a promise! Bible verses about Christ that we have read and meditated upon will come to our memory when the Counselor is with us. The Bible tells us that it was not written by the will of man, "but men moved by the Holy Spirit spoke from God" (2 Peter 1:21b, RSV). When the author of the Word is with us to remind us of what to say, how can we fail?

8

A Witness to the People

When we were watching the distribution of clothing in Jordan, I found myself wondering what it would be like to be wearing the clothes of someone else; how it would be like always in someone else's shoes. Then it occurred to me that this is precisely what Christianity means— eternally being in someone else's shoes.

R. PAUL FREED

In the midst of a passage that has great emphasis upon the needs of people Isaiah says of the coming Messiah that God has given him "for a witness to the people." In the Revelation of John, Christ is called "the faithful and true witness." It is not strange then that believers, like their Lord, in many passages in the New Testament are called witnesses. In every case the believer is a witness. Witnessing is not something we do, but something we are. The first task of the equipper of God's people for witness is not to train them in techniques but to awaken them to the fact that they are witnesses. The Christian is usually told in evangelical churches that he ought to witness, but where and how does he begin? It is imperative that the believer understands that he is not a witness by virtue of training, but because he has had an experience that must be shared.

To witness is to bear credible, believable, evidence to the transforming power of Jesus Christ. A witness is someone who has experienced this transforming power in his life. There is a real clue to the nature and content of the Christian witness in Luke 24:44–47 and Acts 5:30–32. In both cases there is a declaration that "we are witnesses," and that the content of our witness is the death of Christ, his resurrection, and the repentance-forgiveness relationship to God in Jesus Christ. Some questions that one asks about witnessing seem to be answered in these passages: What does it mean to witness? How does one become a witness? What training do I need to witness? How is my life as a witness related to my witness with words? What help is available to me as a witness?

The Dynamic of Our Witness

People become witnesses by conversion. The eagerness of Christians to witness in New Testament days did not arise simply out of a desire to obey the command to "go into all the world and preach." They were eager to share what they had discovered. They cried out to relatives and friends, "We have found him" (John 1:45, KJV). The dynamic of their conversion compelled them to tell what they had experienced in Jesus Christ. There was a spontaneity and an exciting freshness about their witness that could not be denied. Enthusiasm is the ability to convince others. The root meaning of enthusiasm is "in the gods." Their response to Jesus Christ brought them into an experience so revolutionary and amazing that they had to tell it. They were converts. They looked like it, acted like it, and talked like it. They were both winning and winsome. Students of the early church attribute their amazing evangelistic success to this enthusiasm and spontaneity.

All Christians are converted people, but the intensity of the experience of conversion and each Christian's understanding of that experience may differ greatly. There is a danger in insisting that we become witnesses by conversion. The danger is that we stereotype conversion. Conversion may be equated with emotion or change of habits. It is certain that emotion and moral change are both involved in conversion. To some Christians conversion is a sudden dramatic change in their whole life. For some who are nurtured in a Christian atmosphere it is an acceptance of Christ as Savior and Lord after a growing awareness of salvation. Conversion is that experience in which a man who was not, is now a Christian through personal experience with Jesus Christ. Paul says to the Ephesian Christians that the gospel became "the gospel of your salvation." He says that this was when they heard the good news and believed in Christ (Eph. 1:13).

People will not witness with conviction and power unless they have been converted. The timidity and even animosity of many church members toward witnessing to their faith may be an indication that they have not been converted. During a recent revival I conducted, six teen-agers entered into a panel discussion on witnessing. Three of them admitted freely that they had no recall of a conversion experience. They said, "I joined the church." The exact point at which conversion occurred is not important, but one must have the knowledge of personal conversion and believe that it is a possibility for others. To bring others to a conversion experience is the purpose of witness. One cannot witness to something he knows nothing about.

It is natural to expect results from witnessing. Some have objected to expecting results on the ground that it breeds spiritual pride. The equipper of Christians can deal with spiritual pride when it arises. For every one case of spiritual pride in results from witnessing there are hundreds whose problem is complacency. The danger of the Christian is that he becomes complacent about his failure to witness. Expectancy in witnessing is not a matter of counting results. It is expecting by faith the conversion of others as a result of witness given in the power of the Holy Spirit. Someone must have counted the three thousand at Pentecost. When the New Testament says "added to the church," it certainly implies an interest in results. The Savior said to the first band of Christian witnesses, "from now on you will be catching men" (Luke 5:10, Berkeley).

While it is natural for converted men to witness and to expect results, it is well to remember that God never holds one accountable for success in witnessing but for faithfulness. The New Testament does not indicate that "we win souls." No one makes a Christian except God. The failure of church members to witness may indicate that there are a lot of "man-made Christians." They "have a form of godliness." The Holy Spirit convicts and converts. God expects us to evangelize the world. Whether the world is won or not is in the hands of God. Conversion is the initial Christian experience. It provides the dynamic for witness. If a man is not converted, no amount of persuasion or training will make him an effective witness. Jesus said, "You must be born again!"

The Content of Our Witness

In the passages we have already referred to in Luke 24 and Acts 5, it indicates that Christians are witnesses of "these things." In each case it mentions specifically the death of Christ, his resurrection, and the repentance-forgiveness relationship. It is quite easy to see how the Christian is to witness to "these things" by word of mouth, but how do we do this through our lives. At first thought it might seem obscure to witness to the death and resurrection of our Lord, and repentance-forgiveness by living. Indeed, it is much easier to witness verbally to "these things" than it is for them to become apparent in our lives. The New Testament declares that Christians are "living epistles" and that they are to be read by men. The only Bible that many men may read is the lives of Christians. What a responsibility the Christian faces for holy living!

The cross becomes apparent in the crucified life. The cross spells the death of self. The greatest hindrance to witness is self. Both self-sufficiency and self-depreciation must be nailed to the cross. Either of these sins will keep a Christian from witnessing or make his witness of no effect. The world needs lives that illustrate the cross more than it needs sermons on the cross. Christ has an unselfish mind. Paul in Philippians tells us that Christ who always had the very nature of God, "of his own free will he gave it all up, and took the nature of a servant" (Phil. 2:7). In this same chapter Paul cites Timothy and Epaphroditus as having unselfish minds. The early Christians had a holy boldness and courage that can only come when self dies. Sometimes loved ones and friends find it difficult to believe the message of the cross when they see self still on the throne in our lives.

The resurrection becomes apparent in the transformed life. Paul says, "All I want is to know Christ and experience the power of his resurrection" (Phil. 3:10). Jesus, the victim of the cross became the victor on the throne. Paul lived and rejoiced in the living Lord exalted at God's right hand. He says that the same power evident when God raised him from the dead is "his power for us believers" (Eph. 1:19, Berkeley). His evangelistic manifesto to his witnesses is "As the Father sent me, so I send you" (John 20:21). The magnificent obsession of the Apostle was to share the message with all the races of men. The same graces that made the life of our Lord the greatest life ever lived are to be apparent in our lives. Our lives then will witness to the fact that he is not dead. He lives at the right hand of God, but he also lives in us. The very fact that some have said that God is dead is a reproach to Christian living.

The fact that God forgives men who repent of their sin and turn to Christ is apparent in the forgiving life. The believer is a participant in and a witness to the repentance-forgiveness relationship to God. We do not repent only once. The Christian life is a life of repentance. Because the reality of God's forgiveness, on the basis of our repentance, is in our hearts we know how to forgive others. Prejudice against people and lack of forgiveness are great enemies of evangelism. Jesus makes it clear that there is no need to come to the altar to pray when there is something between you and a brother-man. This fact of God's forgiveness is related in the Scriptures to the three sections of the Old Testament—the Law, the Writings, and the Prophets. These three sections express the moral ideal, the longing of devout hearts for the ideal, and the promise of fulfilment in the coming one. The moral reconstruction patterned, longed for, and promised is realized in the life of Jesus of Nazareth. This is the truth implied in the repentance-forgiveness relationship. Our lives witness to it.

The verbal witness is still necessary. The witness must tell how and by whom his life was changed. Self-righteous people say, "I never say anything, I just let my life talk." This is foreign to the New Testament. Our reluctance to speak has its roots in our consciousness of spiritual weakness and sin. Luke says,

"They were all filled with the Holy Spirit and began to talk" (Acts 2:4). Realization is the facts of God made real in conversion. Manifestation happens when Christ is real in the life in unselfishness, transformation, and the moral and ethical witness. But there must also be proclamation. In our lives Christ must be real. Through our lives Christ must be seen. With our lips we are to bear testimony. It is not difficult to witness to our loved ones, friends, and strangers when it is real on the inside and the outside. The witness talks of the joy he has found in the repentance-forgiveness relationship with God. He tells how Christ has set us free by his death and resurrection. Many people are waiting for our witness. Notice that many times in the New Testament "confession with our mouth" is referred to (Rom. 10:9–10; Acts 8:37; 10:34; Eph. 6:19; Luke 12:8; 1 John 4:2).

The Helper for Our Witness

The world waits for our witness. Our witness includes making manifest in our lives and with our lips, "these things." This great responsibility can result in shame over past failures and fear for future insufficiency. If there were no words in the commission of our Lord offering help for this witness, we would have a right to be filled with frustration and fear. The source of power and help is made clear. "And I myself will send upon you what my Father has promised. But you must wait in the city until the power from above comes down upon you" (Luke 24:49). The words, "wait . . . until," mean that we are not to try this task and privilege of witness without the Holy Spirit. The Holy Spirit is a witness to Jesus Christ. In Acts 5 he is called the witness. Receiving the Holy Spirit results in power (Acts 1:8). There is a fulness of the Holy Spirit's power. We receive this fulness by self-emptying and faith. The sign of having received this source of power is effectiveness in witnessing.

The Holy Spirit, our helper, creates opportunities for witness. The case of the Ethiopian eunuch and Philip clearly illustrates this (Acts 8:26 ff.). The Holy Spirit created the opportunity for the seeking sinner to be saved and the Christian to witness. The Holy Spirit uses human instrumentality to create opportunities for witness. There are real opportunities in our homes when some of our loved ones are not Christians. When one is converted, the first persons he thinks of are his loved ones who are not Christians. This was true of Paul (Rom. 10:1). This was true of Andrew (John 1:41). Acts 16:31 has a promise for the salvation of our house. Many opportunities arise for parents to witness to their children, and children to parents. Parents who are Christians are the closest to their children. They know the depth of their understanding of the faith. In families where only one person is a Christian, witnessing is much more difficult but also much more imperative. Lack of love and understanding between family members complicates and frustrates our Christian witness.

The witness may discover that witnessing to members of his family is more difficult than witnessing to strangers. Begin with prayer. Prayer is a much neglected method in witnessing. When antagonism is so strong we cannot speak, we can pray. Look for situations that will make your loved ones more open to your witness. If members of our family react emotionally against our witness, do not become discouraged. Remember that with you they are probably taking off the mask that they wear for preachers and others who witness to them. Many times their resentment and even anger is a sign that the Holy Spirit is dealing with them. The Holy Spirit will help you be wise and prayerful and say what needs to be said for effective witness.

The Holy Spirit will help create opportunities in other social contacts. He uses the church to nurture and train us for witnessing. Sometimes the church helps create opportunities to witness. The church may even send us out with a more experienced witness to help us. The Holy Spirit has given the church leaders special gifts as "equippers" to help us in our work of witness-ministry (Eph. 4:11–16). Church organizations may provide special witness training groups which not only train but actually go to rest homes, hospitals, and other institutions in witnessing teams.

Often our most delightful opportunities come with complete strangers. I have found commercial aircraft a delightful place to witness. People who sit by you often want to talk. Before long you have an opportunity to witness.

The greatest enemy of the witness is fear. Essentially this fear is self. The fulness of the Holy Spirit comes to the believer when he is emptied of self. As a result of being filled with the Holy Spirit, disciples in the book of Acts became fearless witnesses of the faith. When the people saw the boldness of Peter and John, it says, "that they recognized that they had been with Jesus" (Acts 4:13, RSV). Paul recalled his experience and said that he had declared the gospel with boldness. There is a danger that we mistake arrogance or "brass" or self-assertion as boldness. A few perhaps may fall into this trap but there are thousands of Christians who never witness because of fear. Many of us are only ordinary because we have never taken the great witnessing adventure with God. Jesus said, "For whoever wishes to save his life, shall lose it; but whoever loses his life on behalf of Me and the Gospel, shall save it" (Mark 8:35, Berkeley).

The Holy Spirit, our helper, will help us in using the Scriptures in witnessing. In the case of the Ethiopian eunuch, Acts 8, the Holy Spirit began by leading the eunuch to the Scriptures even before the witness was on the scene. In John 14:26 and 15:26–27 Jesus tells us that the Holy Spirit will remind us of his words. A prepared list of Scripture passages used in the same way with every individual is probably not the best way. Sometimes it is a good way to begin. No method of using the Scriptures, providing it is honest, is wrong if it is used to win others. God has no perfect witnesses and he helps us in spite of our mistakes. The Christian is to witness to Jesus Christ. Christ said that the Scriptures testified of him. It is best to use those Scripture passages that present Christ as the Savior of sinners. The witness does not need to know one verse of Scripture by memory to lead a soul to Christ. However, the more Scriptures that he knows by memory the more effective he will become as a witness.

Some passages of Scripture require an explanation for those who are not Christians. I find it helpful to use one of the better modern translations in witnessing. The simple passage "Believe on the Lord Jesus Christ, and thou shalt be saved" (Acts 16:31, KJV), requires an explanation of "believe," "Jesus Christ," and "saved." Perhaps even "on" may need explanation for some. It is helpful to think of explaining salvation to a child. This produces clarity and simplicity. Some have made the mistake of thinking that with some persons, such as intellectuals, one needs a more philosophical approach. However, the intellectual may be only a child in spiritual things. Philip is a good case in point. The Authorized Version says, "he opened the Scriptures" to the eunuch. He explained them by showing how Isaiah testified of the death and resurrection of Jesus Christ, Son of God and Savior of sinners. It is good to "begin where they are" and go straight to the cross and the love of God.

It is wonderful that we do not undertake this work of witnessing in our own strength. He goes before and goes with us. It makes our witnessing so much more glorious when we are so intimate with the Holy Spirit that we talk to him as we approach a witnessing situation. Ask him to remind you of what to say, what Scripture passages to use, and to give you a full measure of the love of God in your heart. Then you cannot fail even though you do not see the object of your witness become a Christian. There is no deeper joy or satisfaction than can be found in witnessing to our faith.

9
The Hope of the People

Could we with ink the ocean fill,
And were the heavens of parchment made,
Were every stalk on earth a quill,
And every man a scribe by trade,
To write the love of God above
Would drain the ocean dry,
Nor could the scroll contain the whole,
Though stretched from sky to sky.

Anonymous

Our time might well be called the age of pessimism. People generally are disillusioned about education, government, social reform, and religion. Youth finds very little to hope for in society as it is. This pessimism has become well rooted in the church. Pastors and other church leaders are deserting the church for secular jobs. Many of these soon are more disillusioned with their secular position than they were with their religious calling. Most of the younger generation in the church have "given up" on religion. The older generation longs for things to be "as they were." Preachers caught in the cross fire of skepticism and criticism have waved the white flag of surrender. Most of the renewal movements have become introverted cells of semimonastic Christians. Campus youth organizations become little dilettante groups endlessly discussing "what is wrong with the church?"

We can only ask with the Old Testament writer, "is there a balm in Gilead?" If New Testament Christians had anything, they had hope. The very word for preaching the gospel has "joy" built into it. Authority and confidence were key words for the first-century Christian message. With the whole world crumbling about them, they were a constant reminder to a fearful generation that "He's got the whole world in his hands." Since they had already died in Jesus Christ, you couldn't kill them. Since they owned nothing, you couldn't rob them. Since self had been crucified, you couldn't hurt their pride. In Colossians 1:23 Paul called it "the hope of the gospel." The triad of Christian graces are faith, hope, and love.

How we thank and bless God for that aged Jew, Simeon, who lived with the hope of a coming redeemer amid the rotten and corrupt society of his day. He lived to see John 3:16 written in the face of a baby and could say, "For with my own eyes I have seen your salvation" (Luke 2:30). How we thank and bless God for the saints named in Hebrews 11 who cherished the hope in their hearts. How we thank and bless God for those saints who went to the Roman arena with hope in their eyes and hearts. The world was evangelized by their dying. Never have Christians needed to rediscover the Christian hope as we do today. Timid, nervous, insecure, tired, and apologetic Christians can never evangelize the world.

In Jeremiah there is a picture of God searching the streets of Jerusalem for a man. He is looking for a man who practices justice and seeks for the truth. The world, too, is looking for just such a man. Christians believe that the man who is truth and justice is Jesus Christ. Recently a great denomination of Christians united in an evangelistic effort, spanning two continents, under the banner *Christo la unica esperanza*. "Christ the Only Hope" must be more than a slogan, it must be the deepest conviction demanding the deepest commitment of our lives. The world can be thrilled and enthralled again with this message. Our message will be called an oversimplification and many of the intellectuals will be scandalized by a bloody man on a bloody cross.

In the synagogue at Nazareth, the crowd was gathered in the simple room waiting to hear the guest preacher for that day. The fisherman, the brickmason, the shopkeeper, and the carpenter were all there. At the back of the room were the poor, the sick, the cripples, and the hopeless. They came to the one place where they could not be refused entrance. The guest took the scroll and read, and suddenly old words, musty with the dust of antiquity, became new living words. The workman woke up and the disinherited in the back of the room stirred, because they knew they were in the presence of justice and truth. The people, especially the common man, will hear today and be stirred if confronted with justice and truth in Jesus Christ. People weary with the unkept promises of politicians; tired of the meaningless rhetoric of preachers; sick of the injustices of the very rich; fed up with the steady diet of success, sex, and sensation, will listen again and believe and be saved.

Hope for Society

Jesus Christ is the hope of society. When the first murderer looked into the face of the first murdered man, there was a promise of a coming redeemer. With all of our learning and wisdom and technology, we have not progressed beyond that first murderer. Every earth's lovely Eden has been stained red with our brother's blood. We have not produced one day in the history of this prodigal planet that has not been marked with murder, rape, injustice, and inhumanity. Socialism, capitalism, communism, monarchies, oligarchies, and dictatorships have never produced one sinless day. Since Eden, all man's efforts to regain paradise have been marked by failure. The common man through all these centuries of human history is "bone weary" of talk and promises. He has died in wars not knowing why he fought. He has watched the rich eat meat while he ate bread and wondered why. He has watched his wife and children die for need of medicine that only the rich could get and cursed the inequities of life. Is there any hope?

The Christian has faith in the future. We know that history is "his story" and God will write the last chapter. Part of the despair into which Christians have fallen is our neglect of the final hope of the believer. Sometimes in the past Christians have become so "other worldly" that they have neglected to be Christians here and now. But our danger today is that of becoming so wrapped up in our present dilemma that we forget that God is the Sovereign and that he shall reign. Christians also know that in the darkest hours of human frustration and futility God has answered by fire. God answered sixteenth-century scientism with seventeenth-century revival. Christians have been known to sing "He's got the whole world in his hands" on Sunday and wring their hands in horror when the stock market slips ten points on Monday. Pessimists are never evangelists.

God is working in society today. Evidences of his working are in a new conscience about war, poverty, and racism. We complain about this because the demonstrators are not Christians. Remember God can make evangelists out of militants. He has done it before and he will do it again. Perhaps if we Christians had been "demonstrating" Christ, the world would be much better than it is. Christians can know they are right with God. They can illustrate the society of love in the fellowship of the church. In winning individuals to Christ and his love, society can be changed just that much. No one can read the history of the church without knowing that at many places the church has influenced society for good. This can be more true in the future as we give ourselves to the lordship of Christ. We can influence the structures of society by winning to faith in Christ "the power structure."

The evangelist is an optimist. He never looks at the world "through rose-colored glasses." He sees men as they really are, but he knows there is hope. He looks beyond the ills of today and sees the promise of "the new heaven and the new earth." His faith is not shattered by a few theologians who think God is dead. He refuses to be intimidated by the false prophets who are experts on raising questions. He believes the incredible. He sees the invisible. His faith is not shaken by a sensate generation who, like animals, only believe in what they can touch, taste, or feel. No man, no society, no culture is fallen so low that God cannot lift it. The Church is the "leaven" that is to penetrate the whole "lump." The Christian sees with clear eyes the evil that reigns today and the redemption that is coming tomorrow.

Hope for the Church

Jesus Christ is the hope of the church. There are all sorts of ideas as to how the church must be renewed. The answer is just as simple as the New Testament, "on this rock I will build my church" (Matt. 16:18). Where Jesus is confessed as Lord by life commitment there is renewal of the church. To put discipleship in the simple terms of "following Jesus" is to find the spirit of the New Testament. The church can have renewal when it discovers that being Christian is being Christlike. A serious study of what Jesus did and said might be the means of such renewal. A great deal of energy has been expended by defending the theories of theologians rather than the teachings of Jesus Christ. Preaching and teaching in the church should be reduced to two great simplicities: What did Jesus do and say while in the world? How can we be like him in our life in the church and in the world?

Jesus Christ can give relevance to the church. The church must rediscover that most of the time that Jesus spent on this earth he was either training men for world evangelization or he was ministering to people with no regard to race or class. He was deeply interested in changing men and changing society. What could be more relevant than this? Talking like a hippie and joining a demonstration is not necessarily Christlike. Loving people and ministering to them with a Christian witness is Christlike. The church through its leaders ask: "How can we do this? Give us a program." But love finds a way. The believer who is Christlike finds his contacts for ministry every day in his work and recreation. Church leaders who are Christlike find a way to "equip the saints for serving."

The church in its search for relevance seems to be asking, "How can we be more accepted in society?" But the real question is, "How can we be more Christlike?" This might mean even less acceptance. It might even mean animosity. They nailed him to a cross. Many writers today seem to be saying that the church needs to be like Christ and that if this were true the church would be loved and accepted. In the light of human depravity this is not only unlikely but completely contrary to human nature. If the church becomes relevant, she will be touching all the "sore spots" of society, and one is never loved for this. To become Christlike is to leave the "safe" way of life and to live dangerously.

Christ can restore the ministry of reconciliation to the church.

Christ came to reveal God, to redeem, and to reconcile. A Christian cannot add to the revelation that God made in Christ. He cannot add to the work of redemption. But the ministry of reconciliation has been committed to us. God in Jesus Christ intends to reconcile the races, to bring Jew and Gentile together in one body. God intends in Christ to reconcile the classes, to bring both bond and free together in one body. God intends to reconcile in Christ the sexes, for in that body there is neither male nor female. That body is the church. This is social reformation in its most radical form.

Evangelism is this ministry of reconciliation: love for people that knows no boundaries or barriers. Evangelism is love that reaches out for all with no distinctions. One cannot imagine Christ dividing prospect cards by color or class. Could he say, "This is a colored family," or "These people would never come to our church." But denominations and local congregations say, "We would lose our identity." Wouldn't that be wonderful, to lose our identity and just be known as Christians? People could ask, "Where do the Christians meet?" We would not even capitalize the word *christian,* leaving that honor for his name.

Hope for People

The thing that made the poor and dispossessed sit up and take notice in the synagogue at Nazareth was "hope" epitomized in a person. The epileptic, frothing at the mouth and writhing in the dust, cried, "Jesus, help me!" The blind man with hands outstretched and face turned toward heaven came groping toward him crying, "Jesus, help me!" The lepers hiding their ugly ulcers beneath dirty rags came to him and cried, "Jesus, help us!" He was hope for people wherever he went. To the demon-possessed man he was tormentor, healer, and master, but he was hope. When he tormented the demons that possessed them with the beauty of his person, when he healed them by breaking the hold of demonic powers, when he commanded them to go and tell no one, he was hope. But they could not stay silent. This was "news too good to keep."

Could this be the reason for our pessimism and failure as preachers, church leaders, and lay people? Could it be that we have no hope like this? Like Israel we have "hung our harp on the willows to sit down and weep." We have listened too long to the "theology of pessimism" and have adopted an almost psychotic obsession for failure. "Look up, brother, for now is our salvation nearer than ever before." Christians have salvation from sin and its consequences. The power of sin has been broken in our lives. We are witnesses of what has happened in our lives. We need not fear anything or anyone. Is this your personal hope? Is it anything new that governments should fail? Is it anything new that statesmen should be confounded by a Vietnam? Is it anything new that we have reached the "stomach-turning point" in morality? Hasn't this always been happening?

On the twenty-first floor of the Othen Palace in Sao Paulo, Brazil, I heard a voice in the night. I opened my window and looked down to the plaza below. There was a man standing and speaking to a small crowd. The second night I heard the same voice. I could not understand Portuguese, but I could understand one word repeated over and over, *Christo*. I went down and with the help of some friends found that this was a Pentecostal lay preacher. He preached for several hours each night. He was vivacious; eyes burning with zeal and sincerity. All through the nights I was there, I heard his voice. Is it any wonder that the Pentecostals are winning Latin America? Isn't this the answer, "Christ"? He was a tormentor, reminding people of the demons possessing them. He was a healer telling them how Christ had healed him. He was a voice for the Master saying, "Now that you are healed, find another and tell him."

John Wesley was cast out by the very church that had trained him. They told him to go to Moorfields and preach. Moorfields was one of the world's worst slums. This man of letters and learning went to Moorfields. In the crowd listening to Wesley one day was a human savage. The man bent down and picked up a jagged paving stone and waited for an opportunity to throw it in the preacher's face. Then his eyes caught the eyes of Wesley burning with compassion and zeal. The man turned to a companion and said, "He ain't a man, he's a god." After his message, Wesley came to the two men, put his arm about them and spoke to them of the love of God in Christ. When Wesley left, the man turned to his companion and said, "He ain't a god, he's a man, but he's a man like God." This is our need, Christlike men, meeting in Christlike assemblies, going out in a Christlike way to witness with hope. This kind of evangelism cannot be taught, it must be caught. Nearness to the Savior will guarantee our catching it. May the good Lord hasten the day.